B
PEC
          Peck, Richard   19462

          Anonymously yours

$14.98

DATE		

© THE BAKER & TAYLOR CO.

Anonymously

Yours

Richard Peck
Anonymously
Yours

JULIAN ⓜ MESSNER

10 9 8 7 6 5 4 3 2 1

Library of Congress Cataloging-in-
Publication Data

Peck, Richard.
   Anonymously yours / by Richard Peck
     p. cm.—(In my own words)
   Summary: The popular author describes
how he grew up in Decatur, Illinois, went
into teaching, and eventually became a
writer, incorporating his earlier experiences
into novels intended to reach and change
young readers.
   1. Peck, Richard—Biography—Juvenile
literature. 2. Novelists, American—20th
century—Biography—Juvenile literature.
3. Young adult fiction—Authorship—
Juvenile literature. 4. Decatur (Ill.)—
Social life and customs—Juvenile
literature. [1. Peck, Richard 2. Authors,
American.] I. Title. II. Series.
PS3566.E2526747   1991
818'.5409—dc20
[B]   91-10067
    CIP
      AC
ISBN 0-671-74162-4 (hard cover)
ISBN 0-671-74161-6 (lib. bdg.)

CONTENTS

PREFACE

When another publisher commissioned somebody to write my biography, a friend was thunderstruck. "Not a *whole* book," he said in wonderment. That friend is in for a fresh shock now if this autobiography falls into his hands.

There's nothing more pathetic than a writer trying to make himself interesting. As far as I'm concerned, autobiography is the reverse of what I do. I'm a novelist, and a novel shouldn't be the autobiography of the author. It needs to be the biography of the person the reader would like to be. This goes double for young readers. From the letters you send me, it's clear you're not looking for the author in my pages. You're looking for yourselves.

Once in a while when the right book falls into the right hands, a letter comes back, saying, "Do you live around here?" "Do you know me?"

Some people think novelists have to live their material before they can write it. "How can you write in the voice of a female character?" they wonder, as if we didn't have to write in the voices of all our characters. I wrote a book about the warning signs of suicide because there's an epidemic of it raging through my readers' generation, and the letters still come. "What made you think of this subject? Have you ever contemplated suicide?" To which the mournful reply might be, "Not until now."

Once at a flea market I encountered a young man selling all his worldly goods to bankroll a European trip. He wanted to be a writer, and so he was heading for Spain on a pilgrimage to visit all the places where Ernest Hemingway had been. He didn't want advice, and so I didn't mention that the world doesn't need a secondhand Hemingway. We have the original on the shelves of every library. I didn't suggest that if Hemingway really had fought all those bulls and wars, if he really had climbed all those mountains and caught all those fish, if he really had loved all those women, he wouldn't have had the time to write—let alone the need.

In one way, the young man who thought he had to be Hemingway before he could be himself was on the right track. Nobody but a reader ever became a writer. But we'll probably hear no more from him. Having adventures in Spain and worshiping heroes is less demanding than sitting at a desk, trying to make a blank page speak in the voices you've created. The fact that novelists need to live in the worlds of our characters and readers as if we ourselves didn't exist may be the central secret of our craft.

What autobiography entails, I'm about to learn, but all writing is mud-wrestling with yourself in an empty room. Its occupational hazards are substance abuse, paranoia, and, for those who can afford it, writer's block. It isn't an elective course you can drop when the going gets tough, and you can't write on other people's money. If you have a little financial cushion from somewhere, you'll only sit on it.

And the whole business is based on listening, though rarely to your friends. Fiction is eavesdropping on the conversations of strangers, and writing depends upon snooping, though we call it "research."

Writers look high and low for voices to tell their stories for them. Since my favorite readers are young, I've never written a conscious line of autobiography in my novels, and I can't speak in my own voice. I have the wrong vocabulary, the wrong memories, and the viewpoint of somebody's father or of the old schoolteacher I still am in my heart.

The voices have to ring true, but fiction is never real life with the names changed. From novels we want a better life than we're having: more adventurous, more dramatic, ultimately more hopeful because a novel is the life story of a survivor. We can experience real life without reading.

Besides, real life is too strong for fiction. There's a high school in inner-city Baltimore that now requires students to cover their own clothes with long lab coats. They go from class to class looking like premature hospital interns. These children wear clothes so expensive and gold jewelry so valuable that they'd been killing their classmates to steal from them. This strikes me as science fiction and too extreme for my kinds of book. The trouble with unedited real life is that nobody would believe it.

I never wrote a line of fiction until I was thirty-seven years old. I dreamed of being a writer, of course, a travel writer. It seemed to sum up everything I liked best: words and going places—and never having to worry about plot lines.

But I became an English teacher. Teaching literature—and especially composition—seemed to be as near the printed word as I'd be allowed to come. In the long run, teaching made me a novelist. In teaching, you communicate with strangers in a shared language. You meet absolute deadlines. You try to give time a shape. These are also the needs of the novelist.

Teaching kept me reading and introduced me to the people I wanted to spend the rest of my life with. It uncentered me because I was the only representative of my generation in the room, and often the only English major. From the first day, I began learning things about my students their parents never knew because I saw them interwoven in their groups.

In the classroom I learned to ask the writer's first question: Who, if anybody, might be willing to read what I might be able to write? I found my future readers right there in my roll book. Luckily, I didn't try to be a writer without some idea of my intended readers.

Seventh graders taught me that a novel has to entertain first before it can do anything else. And high-school seniors demonstrated that nobody ever grows up in a group. I moved from teaching to writing with these two insights. A novel must entertain on every page. A novel is always a celebration of the individual, not the peer group.

I learned, too, that a novel is never an answer, always a question. Only very young writers or cranks or practice teachers believe their words will change the world. Instead, a novel raises questions about the way things are and asks us to rethink our positions. As a private companion, even a friend, a novel can ask the reader's own unspoken questions:

> Is this all there is?
> Will things get better?
> Is it time to stop shifting blame?
> Must change always be a threat?
> If people really knew me, would I be forgiven?

One day in the midst of life I stopped being a teacher and started being a novelist. Twenty years and twenty books later, I was set the task of writing an autobiography. I was dubious. After all, a writer gathers his best material when nobody knows he's there. All novels are in a sense written anonymously, and a writer of "Young Adult" novels is more shadowy still. It's a field in which you can sell a million copies of your books, and some of your own acquaintances have no idea what you do for a living. Parents don't always thank you for inquiring more closely into their children's lives than they dare to do.

A man I've known most of my life recently found in his teenaged son's room drugs and drug paraphernalia. He was disturbed enough to tell me about it, and I waited to hear how he dealt with it. But then he said, "Of course I don't know whose drugs they were."

As a teacher I couldn't afford that kind of self-protection, and neither can a writer. But to that modern father I believe I'll quietly dedicate this book about how I came to write novels for the readers of his son's generation.

ENGLAND

*It was a summer of perfect weather, or
so it was always to seem. The Thames
shimmered with kingfishers above
Boveney Lock, and white clouds thick
as sheep grazed the deep blue
heavens.*

— This Family of Women

A quotable writing colleague, Rita Mae Brown, describes birth as the search for a larger apartment. In hers she wanted plenty of shelf space for books. So did I, but what I really wanted was luggage because I was born with itchy feet and the certain knowledge that real life was going on somewhere else.

This is a writer's typical beginning. If we were content with the life around us and thought we were communicating well with the people we already knew, we wouldn't have to leave town, hole up, and hurl messages at distant strangers.

Other people being born in Decatur, Illinois, seemed to think it was a logical enough place to be. Some of them thought it was the center of the universe, but I didn't buy that. S. E. Hinton was to write that there are people who go and people who stay, and I was to read her words a thousand miles from home.

In nursery rhymes, kings were in their counting houses, and we went with Alice to Buckingham Palace. I couldn't see any kings or palaces around Decatur. I believed books and later the black-and-white drama of movies about New York and Casablanca. I didn't recognize them as fantasies. I thought they were keys to unlock the world, and I wondered how I'd happened to turn up here, miles from anywhere. There was an irony in that, but it didn't emerge till later. Now I've escaped into the wide world that stories promised.

At sixteen I made a trip to New York and recognized it as my headquarters for later in life. At twenty I crossed the Atlantic with a tin steamer trunk full of Pat Boone clothes to spend a year in an English university. Of all the distant places described in books, England seemed the most promising. Somehow it still does.

My first trip to England began on an autumn morning many Septembers ago on an ocean liner. It was junior year abroad from DePauw University in landlocked Greencastle, Indiana. I walked up my first gangplank onto the *Ile de France* in the Hudson River. It was Europe before we even left the port: French food, foreign films, strange smells. An opera singer, enormous and undiscovered, stood on deck singing farewell arias to her claque chorusing from the pier. The ship blasted and moved; tickertape connecting ship to dock snapped and curled free. My parents and sister and our New York hostess, Marie Raven, were in the crowd. Their faces receded as the ship turned in the river and sailed down the bay, to the world.

Ships lumbered and wallowed then, especially on the September Atlantic. By the next summer, when I returned on the *Queen Elizabeth,* it had been refitted with the first of the new stabilizers. An old lady passenger remarked to an officer that the ship was much calmer now that it had been sterilized.

There weren't any private bathrooms in third class on the *Ile de France.* You had to sign up for a bath with the deck steward who kept the keys to the room with the bathtub. When I finally figured this out, the only time free was 4:15 in the afternoon. More trouble ensued when he found out I wanted a bath every day. The ritual was complicated. The steward filled the tub with warm seawater and provided a bar of yellow soap that would lather in salt. On a plank across the tub stood a tin bucket of coolish fresh water. You were to do your scrubbing in salt water. Then stand up, on a pitching ship, heft the tin bucket and pour it over yourself, ridding yourself of saltwater crust. I never quite caught the rhythm of this, and the French dealt with it by not booking a bath.

On the roughest days, the waiters poured pitchers of water on the tablecloths to help anchor the glassware at dinner. By night, I escaped third class and an inside cabin for four and entered the second-class salon to dance away the evening under swaying chandeliers. One bright, sharp morning we stood out in the bay at Plymouth. Behind it in soft folds lay England.

To raise the fare, $165, I'd spent a summer running the dishwasher at George Williams College Camp on Lake Geneva in Wisconsin and wangled permission from my local draft board to leave the country for a year. At that time, any undrafted twenty year old was looked on as a potential fugitive.

A toy train ran to Exeter, the county town of Devon, where I spent the year. There were only ten or so American students that year, so I melted into the British student body. They'd all been thoroughly screened. Even now the British don't consider a college education a divine right. I hadn't been anywhere near such academic competition before, but I was too far from home to turn back.

Our professors didn't audibly assign us papers. The list of individual topics appeared on a bulletin board down a dark hall. When I finally discovered this, my first assignment was, "The Political and Cultural Implications of the Monastic Foundations on the Holy Isle of Iona." Numb, I turned toward the library, and a map.

The barrier between the teachers and the taught was high in the lecture room, but through the tutorial system every student met weekly with a professor who reviewed our work and read our papers for all courses. In that way we got more than grades and comments written in margins in illegible British handwriting. My tutor, Professor Salter, gave his own critical analyses of my papers, in style and substance, the first professional editing I'd ever had, though not the last.

Professor Salter changed my life. I had a problem I'd been running from for years. Though I was planning to be a teacher, I couldn't stand up in front of any group of people and speak. My knees buckled, and my mouth dried. What did I think was going to happen when I had to do five classes a day in front of hypercritical teenagers? I was heading for a job I couldn't do. In high school I'd coped with the problem by never running for student office or trying out for the class plays. Why hadn't I gone to the speech and drama department for a cure? Because the speech and drama classes were electives, and teenagers never elect anything they need. I may have been waiting for a miracle.

Professor Salter provided it. His study was a scene from *Goodbye, Mr. Chips*. He sat wrapped in an academic gown before a window where a high wind blew in from an English garden. "I have an assignment of my own for you," he remarked one morning. "The university is sending out to a local grammar school a panel of foreign students to speak about the educational systems of their countries. You will speak for the United States." There's no place to hide in a tutorial. "I should think a ten-minute presentation will do. Wednesday."

The gray mouse of a woman who brought him his eleven o'clock cup of tea entered, signaling the end of the session.

On the fatal day I put on my best suit, a gray flannel so pale that in England I looked like I was selling ice cream at the seashore. We foreign students were delivered to Blundell's School. Even out in the hall while we waited to go on, you could hear the adolescent audience stirring. Then we mounted the platform. I was the last to speak.

The audience was a sea of young faces and school uniforms, and behind them their living teachers in gowns, and above them on the walls dead teachers, framed. It was the orphanage scene from *Jane Eyre* with an Oliver twist.

The first speaker was Egyptian. But Egypt sent its experienced teachers to England for postgraduate study. He knew all about students and speaking. The students listened. They didn't have much choice. The next speaker was my age, from Finland, willing but struggling against a heavy accent. I thought, what if a version of English weren't my native language? The next speaker was German, and the room went dead. Even to postwar children the Germans were still the enemy. He spoke with precision, and they froze him out. I thought, what if I'd been on the wrong side in the war? The next was a girl from Nice: beautiful, articulate, stylish, French. They loved her, and the room warmed. What an act to follow.

I don't know what anybody said. I was still rehearsing. Then every eye was on me, and I was staring my phobia in the face. A few of the audience were grinning, and I'd already noticed that nobody here took Americans seriously. They may even have been entertained by my suit. Distantly, I heard me giving my speech in a hilariously strong American accent.

This wasn't a big moment in world history, but it was a big one in mine. As we filed off the stage, I realized I was cured. Being on stage was less agonizing than hiding. I wanted to turn back the clock and try out for every class play ever given. I wanted to major in speech, or better yet, speech therapy.

That day opened doors down the years and kept me from defeating myself as a beginning teacher. Later, it freed me to speak to groups of all ages about my books because writers have to do their own publicity.

Overcoming a phobia more common than I knew added an element to all my novels. The only experiences we learn from are the ones we'd avoid if we could. In every novel the characters grow by being backed into corners. In my own country I'd always found a safe haven. Here across the world my worst fear was waiting.

And so all credit to Professor Salter. Did he pick me for the job because I was his only American? Or did he perceive my phobia and decide to call my bluff? I don't know, but teaching is the art of calling people's bluffs.

At Exeter, a university considered almost dangerously advanced, we sat at table on backless benches in ties and academic gowns. At high table, on a dais, the warden of the hall — always a bachelor professor — sat at one end. Matron — always a veteran of the British women's army — sat at the other, with a revolving cast of scholars between. At end-of-term dinners we wore dinner jackets, toasted the Queen, and ate actual meat. Not a soul had crossed these borders without a working knowledge of Latin and often enough, Greek. Still, this was thought to be a radical place, possibly a hotbed. It was, for example, coed.

The tongue-tying shyness that assailed me near speaking platforms fell away on the dance floor. Like Dracula, I was more outgoing at night. I'd been coed since kindergarten. Thanks to a small, fierce woman in a black dress, Miss Van Dyke, I could dance even with partners who couldn't. Miss Van Dyke ran the social dancing school back home, and every ambulatory child from the west end of Decatur attended her boot camp in the waltz, the fox-trot, and the rhumba while in the very pit of puberty.

No British student had been in school with, or apparently near, a member of the opposite sex before Exeter University. These academic giants were social midgets. It was on the dance floor where we American students, overdressed, well rehearsed, and annoyingly clean, broke all the ice. We were the first across the gaping dance floor to claim one another. We danced the first set, five couples with plenty of space around us, while the British, segregated by sex, peered in alarm at each other across the room.

There were other differences between us, as well. The Exeter students had been the children of wartime. I'd gone to grade school farther behind the lines, believing that we Americans had saved Europe and the world from fascism. The British students put me straight about that. Evidently we'd entered the war too late to be of any significant help, and in fact the war had been fought in Europe to save *us* from fascism.

Apparently no two countries teach the same history course, and it fed the novelist in me because it was a good, strong example of viewpoint. A novel is based on conflicting viewpoints. If everybody agrees, it isn't a story, it's a street gang.

In London and Stratford that year I did my first serious theater-going, in a golden age of theater. Up in the seven-shilling seats, I sat impressionable as wet cement and unjaded by television. Though I wasn't destined to write plays, a novel, too, has to speak the right words in the right voices. A chapter is shaped like an act of a play and is acted out without a wasted word or an unused prop, or preaching. The British know more about that than anyone else, that when the curtain falls, the audience has been given the chance to change.

That winter I met the Jones family who lived over the moors from Exeter in Barnstaple. Along with their lovely schoolgirl daughter, Mair, we traveled on the continent that spring, in all the comfort of a Morris Oxford. That was my first glimpse of Germany, which I was about to see a lot more of as a soldier. One of this family's later homes, high on the dramatic cliffs of North Devon, was to be Mrs. Hoarsham-Dark's in my novel called *Through a Brief Darkness*.

In novels, I bootleg as many insights as possible into far-off worlds. I loved geography before I saw any, but nowadays the young in their mapless classrooms can't find Canada and aren't looking farther. And so in my books, characters take trips into wider worlds. In *Those Summer Girls I Never Met*, a teenaged brother and sister, Drew and Steph, are summoned by the grandmother they hardly know to spend two endless weeks with her on a cruise of the Scandinavian ports and Leningrad. Novels aren't travelogues, and I never did become that travel writer, but I work in the lure of distance wherever I can. More important, characters learn things about themselves far from their peer groups that they couldn't have learned at home. I did.

As early as my third novel, *Through a Brief Darkness,* a New York girl is abducted by her father's enemies and spirited away to a house in Cornwall Gardens, London, by people who call themselves her cousins. She'd never been as safe as she'd thought, and now she has to fight for her life in a distant country full of strangers where the rules are different: a metaphor for growing up all on your own, told as a thriller.

In *Ghosts I Have Been,* Blossom Culp makes her bow to Queen Mary, circa 1914, then finds herself impersonating a waxwork in Madame Tussaud's museum. Off her turf, the outcast of Bluff City, Illinois, finds the world opening to her: a panorama of box-kite airplanes and tea at Brown's Hotel. She invites contemporary readers out of their suburban subdivisions and into a world far from their lulling routines. And while Blossom is ready for anything, she's inclined to cast a more critical eye than mine:

> London is called the finest city on earth. Maybe so, but it's a backward place. Smoke from a million chimneys brings on early evenings and blackens the stonework. Much beer is drunk in murky saloons, and they eat fried potatoes off greasy newspapers in the streets. All manner of goods is sold door to door. And the vendors' cries begin long before dawn. You wouldn't credit it, but in this Center of Empire, sheep are driven

through the parks to graze, like open country, though a railroad tunneling underground throbs beneath their hooves.

In one of her misfiring time travels, Blossom even sinks on the *Titanic* and lives to tell about it. There's something to be said for making your research do double duty, and I've written two novels (so far) about that ship's brief passage. In Blossom's epic, *Ghosts I Have Been,* the *Titanic* appears (and disappears) because I'd noticed that every junior-high boy in America knows the history of this event, whether he can find England on a map or not. To generate some conversation during school visits, I boned up on this material by joining an odd splinter group called the Titanic Historical Society of America to get their publications. The next step was to use that material in a volume of Blossom's for junior-high readers.

When I was unexpectedly commissioned to write my first adult novel, it became *Amanda/Miranda*, and once again, the *Titanic* takes a dive. The book's major setting, though, is the Isle of Wight. It's a miniature England clinging to the south coast, promising for a novel because it's a private world with one royal residence, one Roman floor, one medieval castle ruin, all neatly sea-scalloped — a ready-made setting. In 1973 my friend Dick Brundage and I drove and walked all over the island, coming onto the hamlet of Whitwell, which became the family name of one of the title characters. I've never set a novel anywhere I haven't seen for myself, another perfectly good excuse for travel.

My English year was the last one before television and tourism blanketed the earth. Looming ahead was a shrinking world of jet lag and satellite dishes. Young adult books that have transformed American publishing are making inroads on London publishing. In the 1970s the going was still slow. As a British editor of that time said, "We don't want our teenagers to know about your teenagers." But the works of S. E. Hinton and Paul Zindel were the thin edge of the wedge, and YA is now an international phenomenon.

After that college year at Exeter, I sailed back on the original *Queen Elizabeth* to a world of fraternity house, draft board, and a peer group of classmates who were still talking about the same things they'd been talking about when I left. That, too, was a lesson.

THE
NEIGHBORHOOD

*Then later, the town grew out in that
direction, took the land for back taxes,
and turned it into a regular city park
named Marquette Park. They cleaned it
up, put in picnic tables, and turned the
dance palace into a clubhouse for the
tennis players. And they put mallards
and teals and a pair of swans in
Dreamland Lake. But they left the
woods up at the end of it. And a half
century after the roller coaster burned,
that was where Flip and I found the
dead man.*

—Dreamland Lake

 I spent eighteen years growing up
on Dennis Avenue, a double row of bungalows and Dutch colonial houses that ran down to the stop for the #5 bus on West
Main Street. It was a set, hazy with leaf smoke, for growing up
Middle American. Once a subdivision, now an authentic place
with squares of light stretching out across the evening lawns,
over spirea bushes.

Life's first big dream was for a bike, a big, fat-tired, one-
speed Schwinn. With clothespins we stuck playing cards to the
fork of the bike's back wheel. The spokes ruffled the cards to
make a motorcycle sound, a summer-day noise.

We laid out a ball diamond on the brick street, oddly elongated. First and third bases were two car lanes apart, but second base lay down past a half dozen houses. I wasn't a valued player. I'd throw to third to put out somebody at second. This was the beginning of my athletic career. It ended in junior high when I broke my clavicle in a tumbling class. In my novels, when anybody breaks a bone, it's a clavicle. In junior high I was six feet tall, but still, nobody scouted me for a team. Although I'm dead set against autobiographical writing in my novels, I find this paragraph buried in *Dreamland Lake*:

> It was still basketball season, which took up most of our time. I was the tallest seventh grader, and Flip was the fastest on his feet. So we had to go out for inter-middle-school basketball. But we were on the bench a lot. Even though I was the tallest, guys a head shorter could outjump me. And though Flip was the fastest, he had no sense of direction at all and often dribbled right up into the bleachers.

Still, I grew up on a ball-playing kind of street where the traffic rarely interrupted our innings. We played, all ages, both sexes, through evenings lengthened by memory. The white-washed baselines outlasted our youth.

Our house stood on the corner where Fairview Park begins. To the north the park unfolded, 180 acres of picnic pavilions and mighty, timeless oaks. It was big enough to be its own country and had developed like the nation itself, from east to west through good times and bad. In the nineteenth century it was the Macon County fairgrounds with a racetrack. Now in the Depression, the federal government's project, the WPA, created jobs by developing its western wilderness as a nature preserve. The Interurban electric cars crossed Williams Creek there on a high trestle. Later, in *The Ghost Belonged to Me* the trestle is torched by a madman in a scene of high drama.

A log cabin had been dragged to a knoll within sight of our house. It was our first public building, an 1829 courthouse. Abraham Lincoln had turned twenty-one in Decatur that year and returned later to this log courthouse as a circuit-riding judge. To a child, it was older than Egypt. The backless benches were still inside, facing the rotting platform where justice had been dispensed in plain, poetic language. Lincoln, our local hero, was alive in there. The cidery scent of old wood and the dust of the ages kept him within reach.

Fairview Park evolved over the decades. They'd even tried an amusement park at the turn of the century, over the hill from our house, with a roller coaster that dropped into a pond somewhat overnamed "Dreamland Lake." My dad recalled it from its glory days, the Japanese lanterns bobbing over the lake and the rush of the roller coaster. This alone was enough to convince me that everything interesting had long since ceased happening.

At eleven or twelve, my best friend, Chick Wolfe, and I set out to excavate the pilings of the roller coaster. Armed with an old book of local history with pictures, Chick and I crashed through the timber on our archaeological dig. We'd never seen a roller coaster, and it loomed large in our minds. The concrete foundations were still there. We didn't have to dig, and so we sat on them, trying to make our souls swoop. Later, on a church outing to the Forest Park Highlands in St. Louis, Chick and I encountered a working roller coaster and were the first in line. It cured me of all amusement park rides.

But not of Dreamland Lake. I named my second novel for it and used it as the setting. The original dust jacket for the hardback edition is taken from a photograph of the actual place, provided by my sister, an editor of the hometown newspaper with access to its archives. *Dreamland Lake* is about two boys of a later generation than mine who go excavating for the ruins of a roller coaster and find the body of an old tramp dead in the woods. The boys' minds are blurred by the violent fantasies of television. Around an anonymous corpse they spin a fantasy of their own that ends their childhoods and leads to more death.

There's a point about this novel that has dogged me down the years. In it I state plainly that the tramp has died a natural death in the woods. The boys who find him fantasize that he might have been murdered and use this false drama to keep their faltering friendship going. Unfortunately, I've had about a letter a week ever since from young readers who want to know who the murderer is.

I tried hard to make this story something other than a conventional mystery yarn. It won the Mystery Writers of America prize in 1973. I tried even harder not to make *Are You in the House Alone?* a mystery. It won the Edgar Allan Poe award as best juvenile mystery novel of 1977. A writer can call all the shots he wants to, but it's the readers who decide.

As with every other book, readers want to know if *Dreamland Lake* is true. I think the book is true in ways they don't mean. But I never found a corpse up at the woodsy end of Dreamland Lake. The sort of people who find corpses in the woods or who can successfully shoot from the center line or who see themselves as the heroes of their own lives don't have to write. There aren't many writers in America who could show you their letter sweaters. Dreamland Lake's setting is real though, and maybe that's what fiction is: what might be in settings that are.

Chick Wolfe lived halfway down Dennis Avenue. Two doors down from me lived Jane Norris. She was older—the first adolescent I knew—and every beautiful girl still reminds me of her. Jane's youth culture was the one ahead of mine, and their 1940s generation burst into being with a glamor that eclipsed Hollywood. Jane wore cardigan sweaters, back-to-front, and carefully scuffed saddle shoes. The boys buzzed around the girls, driving restored rumble-seat coupes covered with snappy sayings. Jane's generation drifted in a heady haze of jalopy fumes and Evening in Paris perfume. They moved through always-summer nights to the music of country club orchestras. Jane's dressing-table mirror filled up with silk-tasseled dance programs. I sat at the edge of this life—already on the sidelines—only old enough to watch. Not only could the teenagers drive cars, they had someplace to go. They were like adults, but better. Kinder than any adolescent can be expected to be, Jane put up with me. She had no pesky younger brother, and so I applied for the post.

Living next door between us were Mr. and Mrs. Daniels, country people retired to town. They sat on their porch swing, remembering old times and crowing over well-weathered jokes. They could sing all the old songs, including Mr. Daniels's favorite, "My Wife's Gone to the Country." Mrs. Daniels had played the piano for silent movies. Since Mr. Daniels was deaf, they were both clearly audible on the evening air. Through stifling nights I lay out on an old army cot on our front porch, listening to the Danielses replay their past.

With a beginning like this, I might have grown up to write adolescent novels and historic fiction. I did.

At first my dad was a belt buckle. I could see that high. It was silver with his initials, WMP for Wayne Morris Peck, left over from the palmier 1920s. He wore it with an orange-crested green uniform because he ran a Phillips 66 filling station. The Pontiac automobile agency he and his brother had owned was gone now, blown away by the Depression.

In a narrow upper drawer of the bedroom bureau were artifacts. A small bottle of Yardley's lavender. A white scarf with silk fringe. A pair of ruby glass cuff links. Under a pile of much-ironed monogrammed handkerchiefs a lethal Lugar snub-nosed pistol taken off a dead German. Here in the ordinary present were relics of a more interesting, deadlier past. There's a story, possibly only in my mind, that at nap time I reached through the bars of my bed and laid hands on the Lugar, that my mother found it in my crib.

Dad's shotguns lived in a standing stack behind the refrigerator. Though this sounds like a siege mentality, the neighborhood was safer than anyplace could be today. The world knew we kept the key to the house over a garage window. The Lugar was just a reminder of the war. The shotguns were for hunting. On V-J Day, the last day of World War II, Dad stood in the middle of the street firing off round after illegal round into the treetops because the war was over. Not his first. Whether or not the Lugar in my crib was loaded, I don't know, but it makes a better story if it was. I squeezed off a round for the first time on the firing range of Fort Carson, Colorado, much later.

In a neighborhood where other fathers went off to offices every day in white collars and Plymouths, my dad was apt to roar away on a Harley-Davidson, or in a hulking 1928 Packard coupe he'd retrieved from the dump. Like any midwestern boy, my first romance was with the automobile. I sat on my dad's lap, pretending to steer, while his hand rested on the lower rim of the wheel, the diamond in his Masonic ring glittering and giving him away. I learned words by naming the oncoming cars: DeSoto, Terraplane, Chrysler Air-Flow, Lincoln Zephyr, Oldsmobile Hydramatic—the streamlined poetry of progress.

From my father I learned that nostalgia can be an art form. He remembered a boyhood of hunting and fishing in the Sangamon River bottoms and staying out all night. Any swimming hole scene in any of my novels comes from him. He'd swapped seventh grade for the adventure of work. Wearing overalls on top of his serge suit, he hopped freight trains up to the Dakotas to run a steam threshing machine for the wheat harvest. He stayed a country boy in his heart, and his stories mingled with Mark Twain's in my mind. That was one of my first links between reality, or at least memory, and what happens in books. I saw Huckleberry Finn as a father figure.

Like all his generation, Dad was taken off the farm by World War I. When he returned from France, partially disabled with a shattered shoulder, his past wasn't where he'd left it. When he was well enough to work, he turned to town and lived there the rest of his life. Country life was paradise lost to him, which made it sweeter.

I grew up in two worlds. Our house was in the right end of town. Dad's station was in the other, a gritty blue-collar district of unpainted renters' houses and Snap Blanchard's Northend Tavern where the shift workers cashed their Saturday paychecks and stayed into Saturday night.

This world lived by different rules from our west-end neighborhood of careful speech and watchful manners. My dad was king here. He ran the gas station like a club, where elderly men, old truckers, farmers, and railroaders, hung out, telling tales. Large, twelve-year-old boys rolled their newspapers at the station, and so when I was way too young to be hearing them, I began to learn whole new vocabularies. The old-timers had honed their stories with years of retelling. The newspaper boys worked hard on their macho vocabulary and hoped to be believed. I sopped it all up.

Dad was keeping some of the older tale-tellers alive by giving them a place to be every day. Old Mr. Barton, who would have been born during the Civil War, sat out on the running board of Dad's car through every sunny day, commenting on the passing parade. Once when Dad drove home for lunch, Mr. Barton's false teeth, uppers and lowers, rode with him on the running board where the old gent had absentmindedly left them to give his gums a rest.

Dad bent bright red with laughter, and Mother stood at the back door with her hand over her mouth, and the teeth were a disembodied grin on the running board. I'll use that scene yet.

Not all the town characters idled at the station. My great-uncle, Miles Peck, had no time to loaf. Well into his eighties, he was up early and going about other people's business. He terrorized the town in a Model A Ford fitted with a carpentry box where the rumble seat had been. Like a writer, he was in business for himself and considered other people's privacy fair game. He was as free as I hoped adults could be: He worked when he wanted to; he fished when he wanted to; and he said rude things in front of people's mothers. I thought he was God.

Uncle Miles could describe the old Victorian mansions of the town when they were new: the Shellabarger home with its solarium and porte cochere, the eye-popping Mueller house attributed to Frank Lloyd Wright. Apparently, Uncle Miles had built them all single-handedly. The past and the present were a single tapestry in his mind, and the mighty of the town, long dead, returned in his nonstop monologues. Fifty years before, he'd been entranced by the society leader of the time, a rich spinster named Miss Belle Ewing. He could grow lyrical about the parquet wood floor he'd put down for the ballroom in her house on the aptly named Powers Lane. The rest of his language was less lyrical.

As a carpenter in his eighties, he often aimed the hammer at the nail and hit his thumb. Then the air went blue with language I wasn't to hear again until I taught high school. He had an especially inventive word for his own thumb. As his last listener, I drank it all in, amazed at how history had lingered on in this old villain with his white handlebar mustache and his hammered hands. In the long run I couldn't let him rest.

He was to appear as himself in *The Ghost Belonged to Me* long years after he was dead and I was grown. When young readers encouraged me to write a tale of the supernatural, the turn-of-the-century town that Uncle Miles had told me about returned, and the man himself was there:

> Uncle Miles took two nails out of his mouth to make room for the plug. "Well, I am no hand at reading," he said, settling back against the hitching post. "But I don't hold with written-down ghost stories anyhow. They leave a person with the idea you have to have castles and dungeons and like that to attract a ghost. A lot of them stories are German anyway, so you got to take that into account. Some of them is English too. So you

want to take into consideration that they're the products of two pooped-out peoples."

He worked his jaws in silence for a while, getting the plug into a chewable shape. I knew the day's work was at an end. "No," he said, "I wouldn't put any stock in made-up stories, especially them that claim to have took place in ancient days gone by. But of course there is ghosts."

In *The Ghost Belonged to Me,* Uncle Miles terrorizes the town, Bluff City, with horse (Nellie Melba) and trap instead of a Ford. But it's Uncle Miles all right, though I've laid a restraining hand on his vocabulary. The real man would have had no time for ghosts, though he knew every closet with a skeleton in it. Miss Belle Ewing is in the book, too, as Mrs. Van Deeter, "the richest and most invisible woman in three counties."

The book's narrator, Alexander Armsworth, was to have a longer life than I foresaw, but he isn't me. For a start, I wasn't born in 1900, and for another his family lives in the third largest house in town. Since all the houses in my stories are from reality, the Armsworths' stands at the corner of West Main and Pine Street in Decatur. Built by the town's first tycoon, Mr. James Millikin, today it's restored to its original elegance. On the back of the property is a fine brick barn. In *The Ghost Belonged to Me,* it's haunted by a New Orleans girl lost in the Civil War and hastily buried far from her own people, among Yankees. With supernatural patience, she's been haunting the barn loft for years, waiting for Alexander to be old enough to see her home to a peaceful grave. Alone in all the town, Uncle Miles remembers her story and understands her unquiet soul because the past is a perpetual present in his mind.

Uncle Miles inspired my first attempt at supernatural comedy, but he didn't solve everything. I may be the last person in history he got into trouble. As I wrote, I saw I'd created a young boy, an old man, and a dead girl. I liked them, but they were all too far apart from one another, inhabiting different worlds. I needed a fourth figure to draw them together, a catalyst character. But who was it?

Worried now, I took the character of Huckleberry Finn and gave him a sex change. Then I looked up from my typewriter and saw a girl standing in the door of my New York study. Her name was Blossom Culp, and she's never left. In *The Ghost Belonged to Me,* she was a supporting character for Alexander. In the books that have followed and may yet follow, she takes center stage and does the talking. So far, she's talked steadily through three books, *Ghosts I Have Been, The Dreadful Future of Blossom Culp,* and *Blossom Culp and the Sleep of Death.*

In all of Bluff City, she's the most unpopular and least advantaged girl. Her clothes are wrong; her speech is wrong; she takes no orders from the peer group; and she's become by far my most loved character. She receives mail that I do not. From Blossom I learned that young readers will identify most sympathetically in a book with the very people they snub and punish in real life.

On the day *The Ghost Belonged to Me* was published, Walt Disney Productions was waiting with a movie contract. Life was never the same again. I owe it to the town and the times that Uncle Miles created in my mind long ago.

The movie first aired in 1977 as "Child of Glass" on television's *Wonderful World of Disney.* I had no say in its script, and my only contact with the wonderful world of Disney was a private tour of their California studios, to learn that the administration building was on a street called "Dopey Drive."

My mother's family made their contribution to the Blossom Culp books, too. My mother, Virginia Gray, came from a prosperous farm family of Morgan County in western Illinois, old settlers for that part of the country. Great-grandfather William Gray had come from Ireland as a boy, acquired a sizable farm, and married a lady named Roseann Maryellen Stewart, said to be southern.

They built a fine, foursquare house that grew with the years. In a season of bumper crops, William Gray asked his wife if he could store grain for a season in her front parlor. As rent, she charged him a stylish, three-piece suite, two chairs and an unsittable settee. Covered in horsehair, these lingered down the years under the front hall stairs, themselves like ancestors.

Two of the Grays' children died young. The third was John Ewing Gray who inherited the farm intact and lived into his ninety-second year. Between them this father and son farmed the same land from 1852 until 1964, and John Ewing Gray became my grandfather.

It was called Walnut Grove Farm. A vast lawn with mounded flower beds surrounded the house. Standing behind was a summer kitchen flanked by pump and outhouse. An experience of outhouses led me to the most popular scene, by far, in all my books, the privy chapter of *Ghosts I Have Been*.

This superior farmhouse boasted its own electric system run by Delco batteries. My grandmother kept a bottled-gas stove to one side, but she cooked and warmed the room with a big iron range with a corncob fire inside and a reservoir of hot water. My grandfather shaved in the kitchen with a long, cutthroat straight razor. When I knew it, the house was wrapped with deep porches, the staircase made a turn at the top, and the plumbing had come indoors. After the house had passed from the family, I borrowed it for a children's book, *Monster Night at Grandma's House*. It was among the last of the books illustrated by Don Freeman.

My Grandmother Gray, who was named Flossie Mae, had a gaggle of sisters, all with fine names, Pearl, Lura, Maude, and Ozena. Aunt Ozena lived in the Scott family house where my grandparents had been married in 1894. The kitchen walls were thick, said to be the logs of the original cabin, boxed in. My great-aunts, born in the 1870s and '80s, were historic, but at family reunions I'd hang around the kitchen door, hearing their voices blend and banter. Through the crack in the door I heard the sounds of another century. Blossom Culp speaks in their combined voice: never wrong and always precise except for the grammar.

My mother was the middle of the seven children who grew up at Walnut Grove Farm. She graduated from Illinois Wesleyan University, class of 1927, in home economics, to be a dietician. Before I could read for myself, she read to me. She wasn't trying to make a published writer out of me. She was trying to make me a successful first grader when I got there, and so she intoxicated me with words and opened the door to the alternative worlds found in books.

I heard my first stories in my mother's voice. A satisfactory substitute for this technique has yet to be devised. We read the true-life sagas of Richard Halliburton, a gentleman-adventurer of the day who taught a lot of geography as he went along. We read the children's supplement of the encyclopedia: Aesop, Grimm, Robert Louis Stevenson, a strangely surreal story by a forgotten author, called "The Day the Dolls Came Alive," which haunts me yet.

It was also the golden age of radio, which reached us in ways that television has never quite managed. "Jack Armstrong, the All-American Boy," "The Green Hornet," "Inner Sanctum," and a show with a perfect title: "Let's Pretend." Radio used words: to create characters, to weave plots, to invite the imagination. I lay in front of a Philco radio listening to Edward R. Murrow broadcasting from London and a weekly drama called "Grand Central Station," about how life is better in New York. I lay there, dreaming of being a writer, of using words, in London and New York.

Through books and radio and listening to my elders, I'd avoided baby talk and carried off to school a tidy, half-grasped vocabulary I can't find in the letters sixth graders write to me now.

Aunt Rozella, my mother's younger sister, lived with us for the first fifteen years of my life before she married and had sons of her own. I absorbed the dinner-table conversation of my three adults. They talked from three perspectives on the topics people talk about: work, friends, mild scandal, the neighborhood—all the connections of community. It was midwestern talk with a great deal of subtlety at points. A lot was expressed in a look, a turning over of the hand. Here we didn't brawl in the street or even raise our voices, and dirty laundry was never on the line, though reputations were. It was all bedrock for novels. A novel is gossip trying to pass as art.

In time the talk turned to World War II, and Decatur began to mobilize. There was suddenly plenty of opportunity for a town brought low by the Depression. But people were immediately nostalgic for the good old days. Evidently nobody remembered the hardships of the Depression the day before yesterday. Even before we could run short enough to have rationing, the phrase, "prewar quality," was used to advertise everything. The new mood suited me pretty well; I'd been born nostalgic, shaking my head over the good old days gone by.

Dad was issued an auxillary policeman's white tin helmet for directing traffic in the blackout. Aunt Rozella carried bedpans at the hospital through long evenings as a nurses' aide. My mother, the dietician, went to nutrition classes to find us a balanced diet amid the shortages.

I marched into kindergarten on the day Hitler marched into Poland, and I began first grade during the Battle of Britain. Did we know it at the time? Probably. Even in kindergarten we did map-reading. I went into first grade all fired up, with the idea that at the end of the first day I'd be able to read *The Grapes of Wrath*. I made the mistake of telling Jane's mother, Mrs. Norris, who laughed so hard she had to sit down.

Apparently first grade at Dennis School was a large class because we were to be divided between two teachers for second semester. Somehow we saw this coming. Even first graders pluck from thin air the decisions being made behind the principal's oak door. We knew all about it, but how cautious, even sly, were the teachers' attempts to keep us from knowing how our class was to be split.

The day came. Miss Welch stood at her desk, and the new teacher, Miss Logan, waited on the threshold to lead half of us away. I wanted to go. Miss Logan was prettier. Casually, Miss Welch began to read, as if at random, the names of those going with Miss Logan. In the first three names, we knew. The good readers were going. The other half were staying right where they were. Fortunately, I was called to the Logan group. So was a girl named Inez T. As the last names were called, both teachers were almost sighing with relief. The sheep had been divided from the goats with no hard feelings. We who were leaving trooped out of the room, but Inez T. turned back at the door and sang out, "So long, dummies."

One day as a teacher myself, I was to learn again how hard it is for adults to protect the young from each other. I've managed to forget Inez T. except for another incident, in fourth grade. The war was raging into its later stages, and chocolate candy was almost unknown. Never famous for sharing, Inez turned up one day with plenty of chocolate to pass around. It turned out to be Ex-Lax. Worse, I heard somewhere that in adult life she became a nurse.

The great school idea then was to bring the war home to the young. Children are the natural militants anyway, so we gladly joined up. We Cub Scouts conducted marathon scrap-paper drives, though I was slow at this. I kept sitting down on curbs to read the papers. We recycled everything we could lift, and we never walked when we could march. At recess we formed air-force squadrons and thundered in formation across the school yard with arms out like wings, bombing Berlin. The girls sat in the swings, presumably discussing shortages.

Maps with pins festooned the schoolroom, and class stopped dead once a week when we bought our Defense Stamps. It was Us-Against-Them, already our favorite game, on a global scale. I'd breeze home exhilarated. We must have been pretty sure that bombs weren't about to rain down on a town three thousand miles from Pearl Harbor.

But at home, my dad wasn't buying all this drum-beating. Older than the other fathers, he'd fought in the First World War. The wounds he'd suffered were paining him still, and his generation had been promised that their sacrifice had ended war for all times. He didn't believe in the country's entangling alliances, and he thought we'd been manuevered into war to boost the economy and for worse reasons that that. In short, at home the enemy was Franklin D. Roosevelt, the same hero whose picture hung in our classroom.

Nothing interests a child more than adults disagreeing. It didn't even divide my loyalties. I cast my quiet lot with my dad, who'd paid more for his beliefs in the trenches than my teachers had by watching newsreels at the Lincoln Square Theater.

This was an interesting awakening to the fact that adults don't provide a united front. Even before I met the British, I was alerted to viewpoint, the novelist's stock-in-trade. Writers aren't nearly as interested in what happens as in their characters' various and conflicting points of view. My dad could make his viewpoint crystal clear.

Like almost everybody they knew, my parents had grown up in the country, and home to them meant big white houses standing back in the fields. But we were town people. During the wartime food shortages, Dad fattened calves and hogs on the farms of our relatives. After slaughtering day out on the farm, our back porch was full of steaming kettles of coiled sausage and long pans of scrapple. Cured hams hung in the garage through the war years to add to our meat ration, and there was enough to share with the neighborhood.

When he could find the time, my dad hunted and fished and brought home braces of pheasant and strings of crappie and bluegill and catfish. My mother tested recipes and compiled them in volumes. They worked hand in hand in the kitchen, and company was always coming. I barely knew you could buy cookies and jam and ketchup in the store. Mother made her own ketchup and put it up in Pepsi-Cola bottles. We could have fed some small, overrun country.

Dad brought chickens in from the farm, to live crated in the garage till their fatal day. The neighborhood kids gathered at the edge of our backyard while he carried out two chickens, one to fry and one to freeze, and wrung their necks with good-natured zeal. It was a moment of profound theater, and it happened only in our backyard.

In 1974 I began a novel called *Representing Super Doll* with a familiar scene. A farm woman, Verna's mother, wrings the necks of a couple of chickens because that's what chickens are for, and she likes her meat fresh. And I like an opening scene that grabs the reader by the throat.

Mama has her own way of killing. I only watched once, but I have a very clear mental picture. She has a horror of axes and never goes near one. Instead she'll grip a fat fryer by the neck and bring it out to the clothesline yard. It'll be fanning out and trying to work loose. But Mama plants her feet apart right in the middle of the yard and screws up her face like it's going to hurt her worse than the victim. Then she begins to swing the bird in big cartwheels at an angle over her head.

Mama's not a big woman, and along with Dad she's as gentle a human being as ever lived. But that first swing is a neckbreaker, which is a mercy for the chicken. She keeps whipping it around and around though, until the body parts company with the head and goes jumping and spreading feathers all over the yard. . . .

The novel isn't about farm life. It's about something else entirely, but I wanted an earthy beginning for contrast. This arresting opener gave my New York publishers pause and continues to disturb suburban readers. All the more reason to include this useful antidote to a world filling up with Chicken McNuggets.

Verna Henderson, the narrator of *Representing Super Doll*, is a country girl sent into town for high school, climbing down off a yellow bus into another world every morning. In a different kind of novel by somebody else, she might resort to drugs and drink and biker boys to ease her pain as an outsider. In mine, she smiles privately at the immaturity of town kids and makes sure she's accepted by them without selling herself out. The town where she goes to school is called Dunthorpe, the same town of *Dreamland Lake*, the Decatur of my memories. The earlier Decatur recalled by Uncle Miles becomes Bluff City. But I'd prefer it to be the town where the reader is reading the book.

In third grade we had Miss Ginnie Mae Huff, later a distinguished school administrator, but this year, perhaps her first, our teacher. She was profoundly pretty and taught composition. The assignment was to run the length of the page and have dialogue, using quotation marks.

My nostalgia always on the boil, I began: "Back before the war, I used to love to go out to the airport."

Which was true. The airport was a hangar, a wind sock, and a dirt runway with a few Piper Cubs and the occasional traveling stunt flyer. We'd been out there one golden afternoon to see the first passenger plane ever to visit Decatur, a Ford Tri-Motor, giving rides over the town for fifty cents. We sat in our car, watching the thing take off and land. I looked up at my dad, willing him to take me up in that plane, then begging him aloud. I knew he wanted to go up in that plane more than I did, but there was strong, silent resistance from my mother in the back seat. It was a long shot, but then Dad looked over his shoulder and said, "Well, I guess I'll have to take him."

Then he and I were walking over the clods, and the plane was getting bigger and bigger. It must have held fourteen passengers, in wicker seats. Behind us, we heard my mother. We turned to see her struggling over uneven ground. "Wait for me," she said. "I don't want to be a childless widow."

We all flew, dipping for a look at Lake Decatur, trying to see our street, our house. We were deaf for days.

I wrote it all down for Miss Huff, including Mother's quote. The significance of this memory may be that a third-grade teacher in 1943 could assign a page-long writing with quoted dialogue, and get it.

V-E Day, victory in Europe, fell on a May day in fifth grade. Then, one hot August day, an age ended with a pair of atomic explosions heard round the world. In the middle of Dennis Avenue my dad provided the echo, sending his parting shots into the thrashing treetops.

From the war we'd acquired another new vocabulary: a kamikaze/blitzkrieg vocabulary of sudden death and long distance. I acquired a sister, too. My sister, Cheryl, was born in the darkest days of the war. Now she looked up in astonishment at the technicolor postwar era roaring in with unrationed chocolate, toy balloons, the miracle of bananas, sugar on the shelf, and new cars toothy with chrome. We were promised even more: television and a helicopter for every household. There was less said about making the world safe for democracy than there'd been after World War I, which was just as well. It would be several years before we found out who really had won World War II.

The postwar world didn't deliver on all its promises. I'm still waiting for my helicopter, but things could have been worse. At least this era didn't coincide exactly with puberty. Before its hormonal horrors, there was the leeway of sixth grade in a brief interlude of cautious optimism.

In these overstocked times, it's hard to capture the effect of 1946 on boys. After four years, the first postwar cars rolled out of Detroit. We pored over the glossy ads, some of them in color. We collected brochures and hung out in front of dealership windows, waiting for unveilings. The Chrysler Town and Country looked like the best bet; the revolutionary Studebaker was a gamble that wouldn't pay off. Our tastes were conservative; we were twelve. The designs of cars were to us art and status and style and escape. We judged them like fine wines and could spot a design flaw a mile off. To this day, I think of myself as the Hudson of young adult book writers.

My dad was a Pontiac. Losing the Pontiac dealership in the Depression may have made him more ardent. He had a clenching reason why every new Pontiac was merely the best car on the road, and what people drove seeped into his genial judgments. He questioned the intellects of people who bought Ford products, and there was something humorous to him about anybody in a Nash.

Now I often find myself visiting a faraway school out in the car culture. There'll be a boy in the discussion group who doesn't want to know much about my writing career, but he'll ask the old question, "What do you drive?"

I try to ease out of it. To tell him that I'm a carless New Yorker might invite pity.

JUNIOR HIGH

It's no easy task to teach the subject of history in a town like Bluff City. The students think they already know everything, and the parents are scared they'll learn things they shouldn't. Besides, nobody likes hearing bad news, and history's full of it.

—Blossom Culp
and the Sleep of Death

Nobody remembers any more about puberty than he or she can help. It's the dark valley between childhood and adolescence. You wake up one bleak morning, and nothing works. I have a private theory that puberty lowers the IQ ten points, just as car ownership at sixteen lowers it another five. Trying to outwit psychology by creating the middle school hasn't fooled anybody either, and puberty is a far harder passage now than it was in 1947. Now, children of twelve can divorce their own parents, charging irreconcilable differences. Then, even in puberty's depths, we were never more than five minutes from the nearest adult, and that solved most of the problems I write about for a later generation.

On the day we swapped the certainties of Dennis Grade School for the gym, homeroom, and lockers of Woodrow Wilson Junior High School, I little knew I'd be spending my adult life on the trail of teenagers, that in a way I'd already arrived at my life's work. In that tense August I'd bike down to the new school, timing the trip, scanning the blank eyes of the building. Even now in my dreams I've forgotten my locker combination.

No more nurturing, daylong teachers. As Blossom observes,

> The teachers can teach only one subject, so you spend
> half the day traipsing from one classroom to the next,
> herded along like hogs in a chute.
> —*The Dreadful Future of Blossom Culp*

At the end of the corridors of nightmare still stands the truly awful figure of Miss Lettie Jones with ankles like tree stumps, who tried to teach me eighth-grade math, and failed.

We had Miss Swenson for homeroom. While there isn't a lot of content in homeroom, she knew how to establish her authority in these ten blank minutes before we established ours. She timed the closing of the door to the first sound of the morning bell. There was no talking, and she didn't call roll. She just looked. This was the secular equivalent of silent prayer. We were all settled down before first period. Starting the day in fear of her and not of each other put us on the right track.

Miss Swenson spoke to us earnestly about college. There were people in the room who hadn't thought about college, and even the motivated were still six years from it. She said that every detention slip went on our permanent record to be looked at by any college unwise enough to consider us. We believed her. The advantage of a threat is that it makes you look ahead.

Adults then believed in keeping the puberty people fully engaged. From school Chick Wolfe and I worked the paper route we shared, and twice monthly our end of town reported to Miss Van Dyke's Fortnightly Dancing Class.

When her castanet clicked and Mrs. Housley struck the opening chords of "The Fascination Waltz," we boys had to cross the floor and ask for a dance of girls who couldn't refuse. There's no cure for puberty, but this came close. We were flung into the arms of the opposite sex by a woman smaller than we were, and told to make conversation without falling down. We were fairly willing since dancing felt grown up. Certain of us enlivened the tone by wearing bow ties decorated with small light bulbs that flashed on and off, activated by a pocket battery.

In junior high I felt my first sharp kick in the direction of being a writer. Everything in puberty is unexpected, but this was a bolt from the blue. I was shambling down the hall one eighth-grade afternoon when a fearful apparition appeared before me. It was a teacher, not even one of my own. Her name was Mrs. Ethel Snell.

"Peck," she said, barring my way. Picture my dismay. I was fourteen. I thought that while I could see teachers, they couldn't see me back. I was banking on it.

"Peck," she said, "have you signed up for my Latin class next fall?"

"No, ma'am," I said, stunned.

"Oh," she said, "I thought *you* were planning to go to college." Then she turned on her heel and walked away, and I went down to sign up for Latin. A good thing. The study of Latin is the only confidence-builder in the construction and the logic and the rhythms of the English language. Without Latin, the best you can do for the rest of your life is wing it.

But even in the golden days of my youth, Mrs. Snell's back was to the wall. Even then she couldn't sit in her classroom, waiting for the immature to elect her. She had to make lightning raids on the school halls. Latin was an elective, but she didn't tell *me* that.

Then as now, I needed all the confidence I could get. Latin, unlocked by Mrs. Snell, unlocked the English language for me and, in time, two careers.

In the long run, the road out of puberty led across the dance floor. By eighth grade I could neither dribble nor drive, but I could dance. The heavens parted, and Mary Jo Kellems, who was in ninth, asked me to partner her at the Job's Daughters formal.

Up there in High School Heaven, at least as many girls' clubs held dances as boys'. Since you couldn't go uninvited and you could only go as couples, boys knew as well as girls the silent tension of waiting to be asked and the greater silence of not being asked at all. In those pre-feminist days young women had a social equality later lost. Thanks to Mary Jo, I found myself on the cusp of the high-school social round just pleasantly ahead of schedule. Dad drove us.

Puberty needs all the homework it can get, and we got enough to cause student strikes at Stanford University. Nobody told our teachers that memorizing is fascism, and while puberty isn't the golden age of anything, it's an excellent time for rote learning. It focuses attention and asks for no unformed opinions. Mrs. Snell's Latin vocabulary list could fill the longest evening when we couldn't be out on a school night anyway. Miss Lipton made us outline the history text as we moved through the semester. We thought she was crazed. As a result we learned how to outline, and I still know the Revolutionary War in sequence, including the retreat from the Battle of Long Island (see *Voices After Midnight,* chapter four.)

In the music room, Mr. Kenneth Stilwell was allocating us instruments for the marching band. He assigned me the sousaphone because I was big enough to carry it. Thinking it was too big to lug home to practice, I took it. He delivered it to our house in the trunk of his car on Friday nights, and Dad drove it and me back to school on Mondays.

All this while down in the industrial arts department, Mr. Merritt Pease was enforcing a unit called, "Household Electrical Maintenance and You." Mr. Pease wore a long, denim shop apron over a high-collared dress shirt and a dark tie fixed with a pearl. He sent us home to replace all the frayed wiring on our household appliances (our parents' appliances; we had nothing more high-tech in our own rooms than portable radios) and to bring back lengths of frazzled wiring and broken plugs for proof. This alone was an educational master stroke. At the very time of life when we were trying hard to withdraw from home and family, Mr. Pease was sending us back to rewire the house. He never smiled either, and this worked, too. We were at the age to confuse friendliness with weakness. His personal motto might have been the school's: Idle Hands Are the Devil's Workshop. There were other teachers less exacting, but I can't conjure them up. You never remember your easy teachers.

Ironically, junior high may have been the only time when I wasn't dreaming of being a writer. Life as it was seemed hard enough. But my favorite readers were going to be junior-high age, and so what did I learn then that worked later? Not enough, but I still recall how much better the near future looked to us then than it does to me now. In our minds, life would begin in high school.

Aiming my first novel, *Don't Look and It Won't Hurt* at junior-high readers, I told it in the voice of a fifteen year old who's already reached the lower rung of high school. In the second novel I faltered. *Dreamland Lake* is both for and about seventh graders. Now I'm spending the rest of my life answering mail from unhappy fifth graders who'd thought that just getting to junior high was the Big Time. They're not ready to hear that in seventh grade your best friend and your worst enemy is liable to be the same person. I've had to relearn that the young want to read about characters who are twenty-four months older than they are.

Princess Ashley is one of those novels about high-school life that need to be read before high school, for preparation. To attract junior high, I've made sure there's a car on the cover, a powder blue Mustang convertible, and in the driver's seat a girl old enough to drive it.

The novel about high-school life has a built-in junior-high readership. Adolescence looks far better to puberty than it's going to be. But I believe in the novel about junior-high experience, even though it's the ultimate challenge.

We didn't have stories about ourselves back in my puberty. Not even Henry Gregor Felson's *Hot Rod* found me in time, and I didn't meet Holden Caulfield in *The Catcher in the Rye* until college. We didn't need novels about us as much. Our rebellion against parents was allowed only as a brief ritual. And our resentment against teachers was pretty well quenched like the grass fire it is by the end of eighth grade. But novels even then could have helped. We were all too alone with a whole tangle of problems we didn't know anybody else had. Throughout life, we read for the shock of recognition. At puberty, we could have used some company and better role models than our schoolmates. We only laughed at each other, never at ourselves.

In 1977, when I was a writer, the telephone rang one afternoon, a call from a magazine editor with an assignment for me. The magazine was a new one, doomed to a short life, entirely for junior-high readers. "I'd like you to write a short-short story for us," she said, "four pages, tops, and end it with a bang. That's the good news. The bad news is that we'll need it Thursday."

"I don't write short-short stories," I said.

"We pay three-hundred dollars," she said.

"I'll try," I said.

If she'd given me six weeks to write my first short-short story, I wouldn't have found the time for it. But I had only thirty-six hours. I knew I wouldn't be leaving the house, or answering any more phone calls. I knew I'd be bringing my meals to the desk. One of the challenges was that this story needed to be both for and about junior-high people. I decided to use humor of a wry sort, and I sat down to write it my usual six times. It changed my life.

I met my deadline and got the three-hundred dollars, but it was a short-short story that cast a long, long shadow. Since it turned out to be among the better-known things I've ever written, I reprint it here:

"Priscilla and the Wimps"

Listen, there was a time when you couldn't even go to the rest room around this school without a pass. And I'm not talking about those little pink tickets made out by some teacher. I'm talking about a pass that could cost anywhere up to a buck and sold by Monk Klutter.

Not that Mighty Monk ever touched money, not in public. The gang he ran, which ran the school for him, was his collection agency. They were Klutter's Kobras, a name spelled out in nailheads on a bunch of well-known black plastic windbreakers.

Monk's threads were more . . . subtle. A pile-lined suede battle jacket with lizard-skin flaps over tailored Levis and a pair of ostrich-skin boots, brass-toed and suitable for kicking people around. One of his Kobras did nothing all day but walk a half-step behind Monk, carrying a roll of rest-room passes, a cash box, and a switchblade, which Monk gave himself manicures with during lunch hour at the Kobra's table.

Speaking of lunch, there were cases of advanced malnutrition among the newer kids. The ones who were a little slow in coughing up a cut of their lunch money and were therefore barred from the cafeteria. Monk ran a tight ship.

I admit it. I'm five-foot-four, but when the Kobras oozed by, with or without Monk, I shrank. And I admit this, too: I paid up on a regular basis. And I might add: so would you.

This school was old Monk's Garden of Eden. Unfortunately for him, there was a serpent in it. The reason Monk didn't recognize trouble when it was staring him in the face is that the serpent in the Kobra's Eden was a girl.

Practically every guy in school could show you his scars. Fang marks from Kobras, you might say. And they were all highly visible in the shower room: lumps, lacerations, blue bruises, you name it. But girls usually got off with a warning.

Except there was this one girl named Priscilla Roseberry. Picture a girl named Priscilla Roseberry, and you'll be light years off. Priscilla was, hands down, the largest student in school. I'm not talking fat. I'm talking big. Even beautiful in a bionic way. Priscilla wasn't inclined toward organized crime. Otherwise, she could have put together a gang that would turn Klutter's Kobras into a bunch of garter snakes.

Priscilla was basically a loner except she had one friend. A little guy named Melvin Detweiler. You talk about The Odd Couple. Melvin's one of the smallest guys above midget status ever seen. They even had lockers next to each other, in the same bank as mine. I don't know what they had going. I'm not saying this was a romance or anything. People deserve their privacy.

Priscilla was sort of above everything, if you'll pardon a pun. And very calm as only the very big can be. If there was anybody around school who didn't notice Klutter's Kobras, it was Priscilla.

Until one winter day after school when we were all

grabbing our coats out of our lockers. And hurrying, since the Kobras made sweeps of the halls for after-school shakedowns.

Anyway, up to Melvin's locker swaggers one of the Kobras. Never mind his name. Gang members don't need names. They have group identity. He reaches down and grabs little Melvin by the neck and slams his head against his locker door. The sound of skull against steel rippled all the way down the locker row, speeding the crowds on their way. "Okay, let's see your pass," snarls the Kobra.

"A pass for what this time?" Melvin asks, probably still dazed.

"Let's call it a pass for very short people," says the Kobra, wheezing a dry chuckle, "a dwarf tax." And already he's reaching for Melvin's wallet with the hand that isn't circling Melvin's windpipe. All this time, of course, Melvin and the Kobra are standing in Priscilla's big shadow.

She's taking her time shoving her books into her locker and pulling on a very large-size coat. Then, quicker than the eye, she brings the side of her enormous hand down in a chop that breaks the Kobra's hold on Melvin's throat. You could hear a pin drop in that hallway. Nobody had ever laid a finger on a Kobra, let alone a hand the size of Priscilla's.

Then Priscilla, who hardly ever says anything to anybody except to Melvin, says to the Kobra, "Who's your leader, wimp?"

This practically blows the Kobra away. First he's chopped by a girl, and now she's acting like she doesn't know Monk Klutter, the Head Honcho of the World. He's so amazed, he tells her. "Monk Klutter."

"Never heard of him," Priscilla remarks. "Send him to see me." The Kobra backs away like the whole situation is too big for him, which it is.

Pretty soon Monk himself slides up. He jerks his head once, and his Kobras slither off down the hall. He's going to handle this interesting case personally. "Who is it around here doesn't know Monk Klutter?"

He's standing inches from Priscilla, but since he'd have to look up at her, he doesn't. "Never heard of him," says Priscilla.

Monk's not happy with this answer, but by now he's spotted Melvin, who's growing smaller in spite of himself. Monk breaks his own rule by reaching for Melvin with his own hands. "Kid," he says, "you're going to have to educate your girlfriend."

His hands never quite make it to Melvin. In a move of pure poetry, Priscilla has Monk in a hammerlock. His neck's popping like gunfire, and his head's bowed under the immense weight of her forearm. His suede jacket's peeling back, showing pile.

Priscilla's behind him in another easy motion. With a single mighty thrust forward, she frog-marches Monk into her locker. It's incredible. His ostrich-skin boots click once in the air, and suddenly he's gone, neatly wedged face first into the locker, a perfect fit.

Priscilla bangs the door shut, twirls the lock and strolls out of school. Melvin leaves with her, trotting along somewhere below her shoulder. The last stragglers leave quietly.

Well, this is where fate, an even bigger force than Priscilla, steps in. It snows all that night, a blizzard. The whole town ices up. School's closed for a week.

This short piece moved in and made itself at home in my life, as Blossom Culp already had. It came in handy in school and library visits as a read-aloud because of its brevity and the sting in its tail. I now know it by heart. It even became controversial, to my surprise. Male listeners, particularly in the inner city, are annoyed and threatened that a girl could best a boy and want it suppressed. Another magazine, too well known to mention by name, planned to reprint it and then decided it was a "revenge fantasy" and dropped it.

But the real effect of the story was on me. I wasn't used to writing this short. I'd been spending more time with my characters, six times through the length of a novel. I liked the characters of Priscilla and Melvin and wanted to see more of them. I decided to use them again and to extend their lives. At the time, I had a new novel in mind, planted there by young readers.

From their letters I was learning that they hit the local shopping mall every day. So I got on a bus to the suburbs to check out this ominous turn of events. The bus ran from Port Authority to a place called Paramus Park, New Jersey, my vision of hell. Deep in New York City, I'd been sheltered from the truth that America had become malled. When I got to Paramus Park, I began to see the sense of the readers' letters. After all, home and school have become optional, but evidently attendance at the mall is required.

There was even a terrible logic to it. In most suburbs, it's the only action in town, the only paved place, and climate-controlled so you need never confront the real world.

In my travels afterward, I dropped in on malls across the country. I interviewed shopkeepers and strolled in the patterns of the young, practically on their heels. But they didn't notice me there. Another phenomenon: to the young, adults were growing less visible.

I wrote a novel about a generation coming of age in the mall. Their parents and teachers have lost so much control that the mall's the only place left. The novel went well until I came to the end and reread it. I'd enjoyed writing it, in a grim sort of way. That was a bad sign right there. Happy writing makes for sad reading. I'd written a puberty version of *The Decline and Fall of Western Civilization* right here at Sears. At the end, everybody died in the parking lot. I'd broken a rule. I'd left my readers without hope, and you can't do that. I fed my manuscript to the fireplace because the novel was for me and not my readers.

But in the next two years, I couldn't go anywhere without confronting the mall. The phrase, "mall rat," came into currency, and more and more seventh graders acquired credit cards in their own names. The business district of my own hometown dried up in favor of a characterless complex called Hickory Point Mall.

Returning to the original plan, I rewrote the novel as a comedy. Each sequence of the earlier draft with violence and preaching was replaced by one of humor and suspense. The novel became a satire, and my two main characters survived to play the lead parts. I decided I couldn't live through the length of a novel with two characters named Priscilla and Melvin.

They became Teresa and Barnie, and for some reason Monk Klutter became Harley Probst. But they're still themselves, and they're still junior-high age; Teresa is taller than Barnie.

Like me, these two have been living in the big city, and so they come upon the mall by chance, while they're running for their lives. They've damaged the macho of Harley, their neighborhood gang leader (and a locker is involved). They have to go and never come back. At the end of the bus line they find "Paradise Park," looming against the sky in letters of neon fire in a Gobi Desert of parking lot. They go inside.

> "It's bigger than the city," Barnie said. They were shuffling past a stereo store called Audio Jungle. And then past The Tennis Connection. And Shirt Tales. And Milady Maternity Modes. Past a place with a sign reading, CANDLES IN SHAPES YOU NEVER THOUGHT OF.

They've entered just at closing time and have to decide whether to take cover in the department store or take their chances out in the parking lot. They take cover, and their adventures begin as they become suburban pioneers on what I think will be the last American frontier. Will they make it all the way to maturity without ever having to leave the mall? Read the book and find out.

The second time it came out right. I only lacked a title. At a national library convention, a junior-high librarian remarked, "Did you know that any book with the word 'Secrets' in the title goes right off my shelves?"

"I didn't know that," I said, and named mine *Secrets of the Shopping Mall*. After ten years it's still one of my best-selling books and even appears in French translation under the title, *The Intruders of Paradise Park*.

But is it a best-seller for the right reason? Writing satire for the pubescent is risky business. Do readers see that I'm posing a serious question about their values by means of humor and adventure? Or do they read it because they want to be at the mall even in the pages of a book? Better not ask.

Better not point out either that the book isn't really about life in a shopping mall. It's about growing up in a time when the young set up governments for themselves in the absence of any real adult authority at home and school. If I were still in the classroom, it's the novel I'd be teaching just ahead of *Lord of the Flies*.

The real hazard of puberty is that some people never leave it. They go on through life shifting blame and hiding in groups. Now in the nineties I'm reaching for novels to encourage growing up anyway, even when teachers aren't quick-marching you briskly ahead and parents aren't standing firm. A novel always asks a question, and there are more questions to ask now than before.

Unfinished Portrait of Jessica is told in the voice of an older girl, looking back to herself in the week she turned fourteen. Her father has just left the family. He walks irresponsibly away, and his daughter turns in anger on her mother who she believes couldn't keep him. Is it rational to turn on the one parent you have left, the one willing to stay with you and provide a home and a living? But Jessica's fourteen, and a divorce has robbed her of the first man she's ever loved. The minute he's gone, he's perfect.

Her mother puts up with a lot of daughterly abuse in the modern way. But then against her own better judgment, she sends the girl away to spend a holiday with her dad. Jessica goes, planning never to return. She comes back early.

It's told in the voice of her older self because divorce is one of those problems that can't be solved in a single day, or year. It's told by an older girl less vulnerable and confused than she was at fourteen, a girl who's learned some lessons about coping with problems because she's had to cope with that one—like a good many, perhaps half, of my readers. The story begins in anger and ends in hope, and it's called an *Unfinished Portrait* because all our novels are unfinished portraits. Even as adults we have to go on growing and changing our tacks and innovating like crazy. That harlequinesque conclusion, "And they got married and lived happily ever after," strikes terror in adult hearts.

The truth is that life involves dealing with one set of problems so that you can go onto the next set. That throughout life, you have to start over every morning.

My mother and father, at the time of their marriage.

My first Illinois winter.

My mother and I at about the time she began reading to me.

My dad, left, unhappy in lace, with his brother, around 1900.

Third grade, in Miss Huff's class.

Jane Norris, now Mrs. Richard I. Gray, Jr., grandmother of my readers, Leslie and Margo Reeder.

In high school.

The sermon-writer and marriage
counselor, Germany, 1958.

In the first year of teaching, Southern Illinois U., 1959.

My dad, left, with his fishing buddies, 1946.

Kathleen Beller and Scott Colomby as Gail and Steve in the CBS filming of ARE YOU IN THE HOUSE ALONE? in 1978.

From left: Jean, Courtney, Kristin, and Richard Hughes, on Courtney's high-school graduation day, 1987.

A little exhibition of the rumba on shipboard, partnered by Rose Anne Solazzo.

Photo by Ron Perritt

With my sister Cheryl and our mother in Baton Rouge, 1985.

HIGH SCHOOL

At Dunthorpe Central High they've got a club for everything. Chess, Varsity, Baton, Black Belt Karate, Debate, Young Americans for Immediate Social Change, Glee Club, Girls' Athletic Association, Yearbook, Friends of Kung Fu, Pep Club Cheerleaders, National Honor Society, Yoga, Camera Bug, Skeet Shooting, and I don't know what all. The only ones they don't have are Four-H and Future Farmers of America because of course they're much too citified for them.
—Representing Super Doll

Our junior-high teachers drop-kicked us in the direction of high school, and I went forth from puberty without ever expecting to look back. We were out of the neighborhood now because Stephen Decatur High School was on the edge of downtown. This is the time to point out that I came from a town that was a whole community. It wasn't a suburb, and so even a kid could see money earned as well as money spent. It wasn't inner city, and so the government didn't give checks to children for having children. It was a whole community with all the classes and generations in full view of one another.

At Decatur High, the offspring of every walk of life were

thrust together, two thousand of us. As clique-ridden as the Crestwood High of *Princess Ashley,* we tried not to get too well acquainted outside our groups. But we couldn't help noticing each other. The most privileged and prominent people in town sent their children to the public schools because private schools were considered undemocratic. The almost invisible children of the very poor were there, too, like Carol Patterson, the heroine of *Don't Look and It Won't Hurt.* There was even a splinter group of honest farmers who climbed down out of yellow buses every morning, a blending of worlds that happens in *Representing Super Doll.* The high school was racially integrated well ahead of history, and there was no unrest among the races or anybody else because the principal wouldn't allow it.

We didn't know that institutions work best just before they're destroyed forever. Decatur High essayed to be all things to all people and pretty well pulled it off. Ours was the largest college-bound generation in history, and there was no gifted program, so we had no laurels to rest on.

It was an education not limited to the willing. We all learned more than we meant to. If we thought typing skills were for girls planning to be secretaries, we reckoned with a determined little man named Mr. Lamar. Now we learned that typing was at least as important for college survival as being able to compose a compound-complex sentence off the top of your head. He lined us up at rows of clanking manual machines with blacked-out keys to learn our reaches and get up our speed. He gave us endless homework, pages to be executed without a typo or an erasure. Typing came in handy at college, handier still in the army, and essential in my present job. I could have used shorthand.

It was a better high school than you can find now, even in Decatur. They could pass off the typing elective as a requirement, and there was then no driver training. The young will find instruction in that subject without burdening the taxpayers and the curriculum. In fact, nobody is a remedial reader on the day for taking the written driving exam. And driver training as a school subject has clearly not improved the teenaged accident rate.

Those of us not planning on college had vocational training that led directly to jobs in the community. The building-trades boys built a model house every year. The mechanical-trades boys could reduce the internal-combustion engine to its parts. The clerical skills majors could outtype the rest of us. The place was a beehive, and everybody who received a diploma could read it.

On the other hand, we were jammed into a crumbling old structure that in the 1960s was to be burned to the ground by anonymous, youthful hands when downtown Decatur had deteriorated.

The one modern wing was the gym named for the presiding coach. Even then we were expected to sit up in the bleachers, cheering a team we never made, and calling it without irony, "school spirit." Real PE was mainly limited to people who didn't need it, while the rest of us ran laps during gym class in the absence of coaches who (a sign of those times) went out for a smoke.

My friend Chick seemed to have a computer in his head. I'd scraped through ninth-grade algebra as a charity case, and now we were looking at plane geometry. Chick could have done his geometry homework on the way to class, but I had other plans for us. By high school, I had the idea that I needed an A average so that no private college would have the excuse to keep me from a full-tuition scholarship. I needed A's in classes I had no business getting A's in. I convinced Chick to do our geometry homework after school under his direction at the Wolfes' dining-room table.

I couldn't let him do the homework for me because that would leave me defenseless during the exams. Needing what is now called a tutor, why didn't I apply to our teacher, Miss Peters? She was a master teacher, and she would have helped me. But I thought somebody my age knew more than an adult. I got a B the first semester and one of the lower A's the second.

By high school my friendship with Chick expanded to include Don Baer, who provided comic relief, endless good humor, and a cherry red Chevrolet ragtop. Most of our mutual stunts remain shrouded in history, but Don had a fake gorilla head and a convincing long-haired fur coat, and often drove around town as an escaped ape in a convertible, terrifying courting couples down dark lanes. The gorilla gear surfaced briefly in a novel of mine called, significantly, *Remembering the Good Times*.

Television overtook us in those years, but it didn't take us over. The only people who had it were rich enough to afford an antenna as tall as a church spire to pick up the signal from St. Louis. Who knew that television would sweep our lives and turn Decatur's seven movie theaters into hulks? We'd grown up at the movies, matinees at the Varsity, serious movie-going at the first-run Lincoln Square. We sat in the dark, dressed for the occasion, and observed life on another scale. As families we sat in our usual seats in a clear parallel to our Sunday church pews.

I'd spent a childhood with Walt Disney and Shirley Temple. But the studios couldn't think what to do with a pubescent Shirley. Adolescence Hollywood-style was Mickey Rooney and Judy Garland, a none-too-attractive pair, putting on shows in barns. My mother and Aunt Rozella preferred Bette Davis and Greer Garson. Like adults, movies made only occasional concessions to the young. Before I could read, I'd seen Rhett carry Scarlett up that long flight of stairs in *Gone with the Wind* and Bette Davis pumping her lover full of lead in *The Letter*. It was a graduate-level course in Varieties of Somewhat Overheated Adult Behavior, some of it before grade school. I hadn't seen adults behaving like this, but I believed what happened on the screen. It was story telling, and I accepted that fiction is at least as true as fact. After movies, I boggled in grade school at the lack of drama in the Dick and Jane readers.

As teenagers, we had the perpetual low taste for horror films. They gave girls the opportunity to scream and boys the opportunity not to. The out-of-date Wolfman and Frankenstein classics were cheaply recycled for the teen trade. Compared to the horror to come, they were museum quality. They were in black and white as all horror should be. Even now in writing a scary scene, I glance out my black, ninth-floor window, hoping to find Bela Lugosi hovering out there.

Most of the 1950s movies, though, were less gripping. Hollywood was being harder pressed by television than we were. There was that flirtation with 3-D and CinemaScope. Screens grew huge and curved as a taunt to the little TV box. Going to the show was a date when there wasn't a dance, but most movies were pitched over us to adults, though heavily censored for a "general audience."

Did movies help me write novels? The pop-art forms of our

youth become our lifetime luggage, so they probably did help. On film, characters don't speak realistically. They speak and act to reveal character and to advance the story, and there's a lot of editing. And like a novel, however strong the start and finish, the big challenge is to keep the story from sagging in the middle.

The faces of the great stars linger like family portraits. Now, in describing adult characters in my novels, I usually have actors and actresses in mind. It helps to describe real people, rather than imagined ones. In *Unfinished Portrait of Jessica,* her great-uncle, the vast and aged painter, is described as Orson Welles. There was once a character actress named Martita Hunt, the greatest of the Miss Havishams in the filmed *Great Expectations.* I've cast her more than once, as Mrs. Hoarsham-Dark in *Through a Brief Darkness* and in a bigger part as Miss Gertrude Dabney in *Ghosts I Have Been,* the grand, mildly mad lady with the ghost in her pantry.

We sat in the dark, though never on a school night, and let movies wash over us. I believed, but I was dreaming of New York, not Hollywood. Little did I know that I'd write novels that would be made into movies. In the movie version of *Are You in the House Alone?,* Phil Lawver, the psychotic son of good family, was played by a young actor who went on to fame, Dennis Quaid. In *Father Figure,* Jim was played by Timothy Hutton, and his father by Hal Linden. A glamor girl of the 1940s, Martha Scott, played the grandmother. But this reversal was all to take place later, in another lifetime.

Nobody knew that our decade, the 1950s, was going to shape up as a historic epoch, even an art form. Who'd believe that our clothes: Bermuda shorts, poodle-cloth skirts, disastrous neckties, would end up in antique shops? Every one of our artifacts—study lamps shaped as spaceships, circle pins, white buck shoes, the very Fiestaware we ate off of—was going to be recycled at big prices. Everything about us was to make a comeback except curfews and chastity.

I'd have been the last to suspect. Even at a sock hop, I thought the party was long over. To me adolescence was my neighbor Jane's generation, and Jane had entered the adult world by then, the mother of two little girls. When 1950s music came back, I didn't recognize it. We didn't know who Chubby Checker was. Elvis was a year younger than we were, and he only passes quickly through these pages in a later chapter.

Our music, dance music all, was still informed by the 1940s: *Blue Moon, Moon River, It Must Have Been Moonglow.* Slow, insinuating, and, as Miss Van Dyke had required, played low enough for conversation. We got well acquainted with our dance partners, talking all evening, or at least murmuring, and were still sober at midnight. In college we were still at it, dipping at the end of every dance, even on whatever night that was in 1955 when Billy Idol was born.

On Saturdays I bagged groceries at the A&P for the daily wage of $7.45. A good deal of it went for wrist corsages, and I had the white dinner jacket by junior year. Don Baer and Jeanette were an item by then, and still are. Chick taught himself string bass and joined Bill Oetzel's dance band, so that he could go to all the dances and show a profit, too.

If the writer in me was begining to stir, there were impediments. I'd probably already heard that writers can't make a living at it, and making a living was a high priority in Decatur. And though we weren't short of eccentrics, none of them was a writer.

Discouragingly, all the authors in the English class literature anthology were long gone: Emerson, Dickens, Longfellow, Tennyson. I thought you had to be dead to be read. Still, I scanned the postage-stamp pictures of the authors' faces, headlined with their birth and death dates. Decades on, I had to smile at the title of a movie about a 1950s school, *Dead Poets Society*.

I didn't have the wit to ask a teacher, "Why are we reading only the dead?" Would the teacher have known? In adult life I found out why, during a brief stint as an editor in a textbook company. Reprinting the works of the long-gone allowed the publishers to use their work without paying them royalties. They weren't dead; they were in the public domain.

The other reason seemed to be that we were reading classics. But Bliss Carman and Frank Stockton as classics? They're unheard of now, and were classics then only because of the textbook. A few of the non-English majors wondered darkly if they'd ever lived at all. The advantage was that there was a near national reading curriculum then to draw our generation together, considering how many of these textbooks were sold and how many of us could read them. The other point went unmentioned. Past authors raised no controversial questions about the present.

Timeless Mark Twain did, of course, but the censorship attacks on *Huckleberry Finn* were to come later.

These dead poets deepened my gloom. Then in junior year, another teacher opened another door. She was Miss Helen Gorham, and as a teacher she was as good as you can get, at her best with poetry. Though she didn't light a fire under everybody, I was smoldering tinder. Poetry isolated images and handed them over. Poetry has to say a lot in a line, and so does a novel.

We'd been reading a poet still in the anthologies then,

Vachel Lindsay. Though he was dead, he'd come from the next town down Route 36, Springfield. He'd put that town into a fine poem called "Abraham Lincoln Walks at Midnight." Even among poets, Lindsay had been an eccentric. In the 1920s he'd performed his own poetry about silent movie stars and Governor Altgeld of Illinois ("The Eagle That Is Forgotten") and an epic inspired by the first of the long-distance automobile races, "The Santa Fe Trail." He'd woven the motifs of American life and pop art into poetry. Maybe you could be a writer even though you lived in modern times (Lindsay had died only four years before I was born), even though you were from Illinois.

One day Miss Gorham announced that Vachel Lindsay's sister would present an evening of her brother's work at the local college. I went and took my mother. A woman strode onto the stage of Albert Taylor Hall at Millikin University. She was Olive Lindsay Wakefield, in her eighties; her brother had been born in 1878. She wore an old beaded evening gown and had the poet's hawkish profile. In his day, he'd practiced what's now called performance art, acting it out, moving with it in a muscular way; he was sometimes accompanied by percussion. She was old but inspired, and when she launched into "The Santa Fe Trail," she began first to jig and then to dance. It was one of the more curious footnotes in the history of modern poetry, and it ought to have been filmed. Her beaded skirts swirled up, and she was wearing tennis shoes.

A few weeks later, I was at her door. On a blistering Sunday afternoon, we were out for a family drive. Even a seventeen year old occasionally took Sunday afternoon drives with the family then. It may have had something to do with not having your own car. I said I'd like to go to Springfield and call on Mrs. Wakefield, and my family sat out in the car under a shade tree while I went up to the door of the Lindsay house. Today, it's a museum to the poet. Then it was the home of a lonely old lady. I was unclear about why I was there. She opened the door, and I saw her poet brother's face again.

Then I was in the back parlor across a heaped library table from her. I was too young to see how much she needed company. My mind wandered all over the house. A famous poet had lived here, raised his children here, died in one of these rooms. The house had a longer history. A local story had it that Abraham Lincoln had met Mary Todd in this house. My head pounded with history and poetry and all kinds of things just out of reach.

But Mrs. Wakefield had her own agenda. When someone young came to the door, she saw hope. Her fear was that after her time her brother would be forgotten. I'd read the only biography of him, by Edgar Lee Masters, another Illinois poet we'd studied. His *Spoon River Anthology* was about Petersburg, the next town north of Springfield. A copy of his Lindsay biography lay on the table.

"Take it up," Mrs. Wakefield said. When I opened the book, I saw that all but one of the pages had been ripped out. Adding to the effect of this vandalism, the only page left was the photograph of Lindsay's death mask.

"I have torn out every page on which a lie about my brother appeared. Never set a lesser poet to write the biography of a greater one."

Before I left that afternoon, she said she hoped that somebody in my generation would find a way to keep alive her brother's spirit. But somehow life doesn't move in a line that direct. As a teacher, I had indifferent success in promoting his work to students, and when another biography of him was written, it wasn't by me.

On the other hand, over and over in my novels, very young people encounter very old ones, often wise and eccentric, with wisdom to share that's taken a lifetime to gather. Uncle Miles, of course, and then Lucius Pirie in *Unfinished Portrait of Jessica*. More often, they're old women living in houses cluttered with the past. Madame Malevich in *Are You in the House Alone?*, Miss Dabney in *Ghosts I Have Been*, Polly Prior in *Remembering the Good Times*, Grandmother Livingston in *Father Figure*. It may have been Mrs. Wakefield I've kept alive, and not her brother.

Then we were seniors with college on the horizon. They don't make senior years like that anymore. At the far end, in June, a senior prom in the gym with parents watching from the bleachers. And all of us at home by one A.M. in our own beds.

The big moment for me fell on the first day of the year, in college-prep English, taught by Miss F. We'd had three years to dread her, but if you aspired to college, there was no avoiding her. On that September morning, she entered the room, looked us over, and spoke memorable words.

"I can get all of you in this room into the colleges of your choices . . . or I can keep you out."

There wasn't a nonbeliever in the bunch, certainly not me. But I'd fallen into bad habits as an English student. I'd grown accustomed to receiving A's on my compositions, and you don't learn much from an A. I thought I needed those A's, and I'd thought I deserved them in English class. When Miss F. returned my first paper, there was no grade on it at all. Instead, written across the page were words still carved on my heart: "Never express yourself again on my time. Find a more interesting topic."

Well, I was seventeen. I didn't know what a more interesting topic than me would be. I actually went to the woman and asked, "What would a more interesting topic be?"

"Almost anything," she replied.

That led me to the library, a place I'd successfully avoided up until then, in search of subject matter that was not me. All these years later, I'm still looking for it.

Miss F. didn't teach creative writing, and wouldn't. She knew the danger of inspiration coming ahead of grammar. She knew that without the framework for sharing, ideas are nothing. She knew that writing is communication, not self-expression, and that you'd better have your reader in mind on every line (especially if your reader was Miss F.).

Under her we learned that the only real writing is rewriting, that deadlines are to be met, not extended. What she really liked were footnotes. That made a writer out of me. A novel, too, has to be documented on every page, not with footnotes, but in the realities of the readers.

By college freshman year, I was already praising her name. Far more than any professor to come, she shaped the writer in me. There are lessons you can learn only in the heart of adolescence. And what you can get away with in high school becomes your lifelong burden.

Never mind the demands of other teachers, she kept us busy till June, getting us ready. The University of Illinois down the road at Champaign was then notorious for eliminating the weaker third of its freshman class by means of the composition course. Miss F. didn't want that on her record.

There were two more landmarks that spring. In March, I received the scholarship I'd been chasing. It was an Edward Rector Scholarship to DePauw University. The other was my eighteenth birthday. We boys celebrated that birthday by registering with the local draft board. Since President Carter, eighteen-year-old boys again have to do that, but then it was different. After high-school graduation, we were to be called up for two years of army duty, war or peace. (The navy, air force, and marines didn't draft because they had plenty of volunteers trying to avoid the army.) At the draft board's discretion, we could apply for annual deferments to get through college, putting off the inevitable for four years, with luck. There was a war on at the time. From June 25, 1950, we were fighting in Korea. The fabled postwar period we'd waited for through grade school had lasted not quite five years.

Then it was time to go to Lindquist's photography studio to have our senior pictures taken, and to order our caps and gowns. We were still doing homework the night before that heavily chaperoned prom.

And so in my novels I dare never approach those fatal words, "When I was your age, . . ." for in all the ways that count, I never really was. If I could master time travel and send the generation of the nineties to the schools of the 1950s, I would. But then you wouldn't need these novels about finding your own way through the present.

When I was young, adults ran the world. When I was grown, the young were running it. On my worst days, I think I lost out twice. I didn't, of course. I'm glad nobody ever asked me whether I wanted to learn or not, whether I wanted to be a member of my own family or not. And I'm glad I was young when you could be a part-time conformist and get away with it.

Memory is the great editor, and what I remember best about being young may never have happened. I don't remember graduation at all, except that I'd collected just enough B's on my transcript, in elective courses and that one from Miss Peters, to eliminate the danger of being made class orator.

Instead, I remember something else, one final thing. On a brilliant June day a boy in our class died, in a swimming accident. Even those of us who didn't know him very well went to the funeral. It was more than just another event thrust into a week of yearbooks and rented robes. Did we know we could die? Surely not—we were adolescents. But now this challenge. On our way to the world, we filed past the coffin of one of our own. Now you see death earlier, in drugs and gangs and on the highway with the alcohol and gasoline your parents pay for, in the suicides of seventh graders. But we looked our first on death, a quick glance and away, on the week we were being spilled into the world. What did we say to each other to soften this blow, to deny it? I can't remember, and now I want to know.

After graduation, we thought we'd left adolescence behind. College was to be the Big Time, as high school had seemed in junior high. The Big Time was always unreachably ahead, and to some of us it still is. By then we'd have tired of being called teenagers, but I wasn't destined to make a clean break. Decades later, for a very different generation of the young I was to write something called:

A Teenager's Prayer

Oh, Supreme Being, and I don't mean me:
Give me the vision to see my parents as human beings
because if they aren't, what does that make me?

Give me vocabulary because the more I say *you know,* the less anyone does.

Give me freedom from television because I'm beginning to distrust its happy endings.

Give me sex education to correct what I first heard from thirteen year olds.

Give me homework to keep me from flunking Free Time.

Give me a map of the world so I may see that this town and I aren't the center of it.

Give me the knowledge that conformity is the enemy of friendship.

Give me the understanding that nobody ever grows up in a group, so I may find my own way.

Give me limits so I will know I'm loved.

And give me nothing I haven't earned so that this adolescence doesn't last forever.

Amen

COLLEGE AND THE ARMY: TWO EDUCATIONS

> *In the sunny days of autumn our professors held class outdoors on the campus grounds as the brilliant leaves fell around us.*
> —Unfinished Portrait of Jessica

I got into the college of my choice—there's a phrase that still rings with meaning. I needed the scholarship first, and I saw in my mind a small, selective college with white columns, blue-and-gold football afternoons, and a bell tolling from a tower. A controlled environment. It was DePauw University, set among the brilliant leaves of rolling Indiana.

Now in the nineties, our young adult novels rarely follow their characters to college. In her unfinished portrait, Jessica is revealed at the end as a college girl looking back on her younger self, but we learn more about who she was than who she's becoming.

Maybe we don't have a literature about college now because it isn't so different from high school anymore. But college used to be the place where you first reaped what you'd sown in high school.

Across the picture-book campus in Asbury Hall, Dr. Andrew Crandall was still at his post, teaching American history. His round, glinting glasses examined the past, and there were scholarly looking stains on his ties. His wife called herself a widow, having lost her husband in the Civil War. My freshman composition professor was no match for Miss F., but he graded down my first composition because there wasn't enough variation in sentence lengths. I'm still careful about that.

Nobody could have a car at that college, a real advantage to those of us who couldn't afford one, and drinking led more or less directly to expulsion. Rumor had it that the Deke fraternity boys drank like fish, but we weren't Dekes. Strangely, the college was famous for its brisk social life.

Dazzling girls too blonde to believe descended the Pi Phi staircase to claim their wrist corsages. We floated off to the Union Building where you could dance from the ballroom out through French doors onto a starlit terrace. Nice girls didn't drink. Nice girls didn't do anything.

We must have been on the dance floor the night James Dean died in his Porsche Spyder on the way to the road races in Salinas, California. We didn't know him then, nor that he'd be the symbol, even the martyr for our generation. We didn't think we had any identity as a generation.

Through a time warp, in the fall of 1988 I was to meet a girl at her high school. She hadn't come into the library where I was signing books because she wanted to meet a writer. Giving me a long look, she said, "I'm not sure how old you are."

I was in no hurry to tell her, but then she said, "Would you be the age of James Dean?" For a moment I couldn't think who she meant, but she was opening her billford, and there was a brooding picture of him, taken long before her lifetime. Yes, I'd be his age. Now he'd have been mine.

"Why?" I asked her.

"I love him," she said, and went away.

Did we? I can't remember. We saw his movies after his death. As it happened, he starred in the only one that was about our generation. We'd been hammered by the standards of teachers and parents, stunned into obedience, handed rule books even for occasions that never arose. We didn't drop out of school for a year to find ourselves for fear the draft board would find us first. Reminded every morning of what we owed others and our country, threatened academically, socially, sexually, militarily, we were told how lucky we were to be young when we were. The movie was called *Rebel Without a Cause.*

Every young generation has its own style in pretending to be older. Denied strong drink, fast cars, and loose women, we at the Delta Chi house impersonated grown men. Our chapter meetings were meetings of the board, and a good many of us went on to be CEOs and lawyers. We played a lot of bridge and conducted coffee hours after football games. On Fathers Weekend, we entertained our dads in a room full of wing tips, rep ties, firm handshakes, and eye contact. You could barely tell the generations apart. If this sounds too heavy, we could burst into song at any moment, and often did. Even the tone-deaf weren't excused from song practice around the battered baby grand. Once the house caught fire, and while we raced around, trying to save our skins and our wardrobes, one group lost valuable time futilely trying to upend the baby grand and get it out the door.

We were also a bunch of palpitating adolescents. Decorating our rooms were traffic signs that ought to have been returned to the roadside, and on one occasion a barnyard animal. We'd have liked to have been wild and crazy guys, but something profound happened to us all midway through our freshman year. A senior in our house had let his grades slip below the college average. This tripped a wire, and the administration informed his hometown draft board. Instead of second-semester senior year, he was doing basic training at Fort Leonard Wood.

We already kept study hours. We couldn't use the phone in our own house between dinner and nine o'clock. Now we set up study groups. Juniors edited the comp assignments of freshmen. We gave each other mock exams on the nights before exams. We burned the midnight oil.

There was a rumor that the Dekes had rolled up their house-mother in a mattress and dropped her out a window of their fraternity house. Under our kind of pressure, we needed a rumor like that, but we didn't believe it. (In 1988 the Dekes (Delta Kappa Epsilon) were to field successfully two of their brothers as the president and the vice president of the United States, one of them from the DePauw chapter. Those Dekes are always up to something.)

I appear to portray my college life as a cross between a full-security prison and a musical comedy. Close enough, and it makes a point about late adolescence. We were scheduled and ruled from above as no later generation was to be. But most of our rules and codes came from us. We wanted an even tighter framework than our adults had thought of. We wanted sure things in an uncertain world.

When history revised us, we were called the silent generation. Far from it. You can be articulate without shouting anybody down or banning alternate views from the campus. We were verbal to a fault and could debate all night without ever saying "like" or "you know." The young Democrats of the Jackson Club were on the Young Republicans' case through both Eisenhower elections. And there was nothing like the draft to keep our eyes on world events. The living rooms of the fraternity house were awash with Indianapolis *Stars*.

We overgoverned ourselves through every sort of campus council. Every year the fraternities and sororities held something high-minded called "Greek Week." It always ended with a speaker from outside condemning our conformity while we, the sponsors, listened with respect and then gave a coffee hour. Except in the heat of party politics, we were conditioned to examine all sides of an issue and to lose gracefully, which made us solid citizens, so-so tennis partners, and fatal parents. We debated only among ourselves. The demands of our elders and later our children were nonnegotiable.

For me, the important changes occurred far off in England. But DePauw had made that happen, too, with a foreign study program ahead of its time. I returned with the edge off my midwestern dialect and tweeds too heavy for Rush Week. It was to be a senior year to warm Miss F.'s heart. For two semesters I played catch-up ball, trying to work in all the education courses I should have had in junior year to qualify for a teaching credential, along with practice teaching.

This isn't the place to condemn the education department

courses we had to take. That comes in a later chapter when I was to learn that those courses didn't prepare me for a minute of classroom survival. Our professors were more cloistered than we were from the realities of public schools and being young.

We don't write novels of college now. The college experience has sunk too low, epitomized by the parent quoted in the April 24, 1989, issue of *Time*:

> I grew up in a poor family with four kids, and we had no extras. There's no way my kids are going to be like that. We want to make sure that if they're not good athletes or smart academically, they can still go to college.

And so the Depauw I remember figures less in my books than the experiences before and after it. But those years count. At the end of adolescence, we still thought that group identity would mask personal inadequacy. We believed in badges and belonging; on the threshold of adulthood, we clung together. My novels are about that, about how nobody grows up in a group and how all the governments the young set up for each other are devised to delay. Pretending to be an adult is the slow way to get there.

Only one of my novels rises directly out of college memories, *New York Time*, written for adult readers who share my recollections of those last, prerevolutionary days. It's a comedy, since nobody has ever taken very seriously the problems of whatever generation I happen to be.

On the first page, a coed of my generation is in the bleachers:

> Up there in the cheering section, palpitating amid the last of the felt skirts and cinch belts, I first scouted Mr.

Right dribbling down the court in the last of the crew-
cuts and the glasses taped to the temples.

Their tale deals with the decline and fall of a "perfectly ser-
viceable marriage" contracted at a recognizable college. Tom
and Barbara are conditioned to believe in marriage as a solution if it includes a center-hall colonial in the right Chicago
suburb. When they move to New York, their old beliefs erode
at the same rate as the city itself.

The publishing history of *New York Time* was itself a comedy of errors. The book sank, though not without a trace. The
Boston Public Library review compared me to Erma Bombeck.
The British reviewers were puzzled by all the references to
Americana: Tri-Delts pinned to Sigma Nus and Twinkies for
dessert. Reviewers on both sides of the Atlantic accused me of
writing it for the film rights, which were never sold.

Perversely, this is my own favorite book. I prefer comedy, as
long as it has a surgical edge, and this book brought me the
best of reader mail. Letters still come from people who've
somehow discovered *New York Time* and wonder if I went to
college with them. It's found friends who didn't think anybody
else remembered a vanished world and how it shaped a certain generation.

Dr. Ralph Bunche spoke at graduation for the Class of '56,
foretelling the civil rights struggles to come. But young, we
thought the future would be like the present with the same
people in charge. The world we entered had less than a decade to run.

We went on to military service or to the jobs we could get
while waiting for our numbers to come up. My draft board
dragged its feet, and I needed a job. No school would hire me

until I'd done my duty. Fewer than ten years later young men went into teaching in order to avoid the draft, but all the systems were in free-fall by then. Young women slipped into teaching jobs ahead of us draftees and were thus two years ahead on the tenure track. Another forgotten pre-feminist advantage now lost.

Waiting to be drafted, I got a job as "executive trainee" for the telephone company, of all outfits. It paid for a four-year-old Pontiac Catalina, cream over turquoise. The job was a search-and-destroy mission to remove all pay phones from the illegal businesses of Gary, Indiana. State law decreed that a pay phone had to be within sight of the front door of a business establishment. There were pay phones in bedrooms all over Gary. Nothing in the college curriculum had prepared me for organized crime, off-track betting, and houses of prostitution, but I assumed this was only an aberration in life's plan, and it turned out to be. Anyway, I had a car to pay off.

Everybody who was ever in the army remembers the day he went in and the day he got out. With flawless timing, I was inducted on the day Russia crushed the Hungarian revolution. In basic training, we were assured that we'd be in the first wave and that we had life expectancies of eleven weeks, tops. But America didn't intervene, which may be why I'm writing these words now.

I waited in the Decatur train station for the four A.M. train, the first of many early mornings, with a copy of *Moby Dick*. Somehow I thought I'd be spending the next two years with nobody to talk to. I don't know why I thought this. Presumably all the able-bodied nonfelons of my generation were going where I was going.

We did basic training in a Colorado winter at Fort Carson,

not the sort of experience an all-volunteer army would put up with. On bivouac we did the fifty-mile march in full pack up a mountain not much lower than Pike's Peak and slept in shelter halves at this elevation on January nights, safe at last from the sergeants. We ran our morning miles in time to be at the firing range by two-thirty A.M. and then stood huddled, dreaming of heat, waiting for enough daylight to fire. I lost twenty-five pounds and kept them off for twenty-five years.

In basic, we fell into two distinct generations. The farm and inner-city boys tended to go in at eighteen after high school. The college grads were twenty-two and had been institutional-ized before. At once, I began to learn the uses of a college edu-cation. We who'd been to college knew how to take multiple-choice exams far more subtle than the army could devise. Every time we were quizzed, we came out in the top half. After advanced basic at Fort Bliss, Texas, those in the lower half were shipped out to drive trucks in Korea. President Eisen-hower had put a stop to the Korean conflict in 1953. Still, no-body wanted to go there. Advanced basic had been mainly classroom study on the operation of an already obsolete guided missile, so we top scorers were aimed at missile in-stallations in Germany. Then as now, Europe sounded better to me than anywhere else. But hunkering outdoors in German winter weather beside a nonfunctional guided missile didn't sound good at all. The army's the place where you learn to go into business for yourself.

When we sailed for Bremerhaven, I managed to misplace my own records in transit. At Ansbach in what was then West Ger-many, I reported to the dayroom as a clerk/typist. It was the army's own oversight that I hadn't been sent to clerk/typist school, not that I needed it.

In that dayroom of the former Nazi barracks at Ansbach, I learned the advantages of literacy. Where I'd been, literacy was a given. But the army was a vast, barely literate power structure that ran on paperwork. By the time they learned I hadn't been to clerk/typist school, I was cutting stencils for the daily report. Money is meaningless in the army, but a sit-down job by a warm stove is riches.

It took a while to get the hang of it. The army does things to the English language I hadn't known you could do. Army language is meant to conceal, not reveal.

One morning early in my career I was sitting in combat boots at the typewriter, trying to read a copy of *Barchester Towers* propped in the desk drawer. Into the office came a sergeant with a raw recruit. He was a nineteen-year-old kid big as a house, and he had trouble written all over him. His sergeant applied to mine, saying, "We got to get this young trooper home."

It seemed that the boy's girlfriend back home found herself pregnant and had high hopes for a hasty wedding.

Getting permission to go home for any reason was virtually unheard of. My father was soon to fall dangerously ill and undergo emergency surgery, but I was denied compassionate leave. But the sexual aspect of the young trooper's dilemma excited his sergeant and possibly mine. They agreed that he had to get home, but paperwork was involved, and they didn't know how to phrase it. They did their best while I listened. Some of their phrasing would do neither in a report nor on this page. I let them sweat, and the young trooper was sweating buckets.

Then I said, "Sergeant, how about: 'Permission to travel stateside to marry the mother of my unborn child'?"

Three heads turned my way, and my sergeant said, "Say that one more time." I did. He copied out the words onto the travel orders, checked them over, and said, "I think I've got it."

As the unwed father-to-be was led away, to an altar, it dawned on me that there were advantages for English majors. Pre-med is still a better bet, but the army was an early proof that being able to compose on cue is a rarer skill than I knew. From then on I was the word doctor around that office, and it happens that the first words I ever wrote for publication of a sort were, "Permission to travel stateside to marry the mother of my unborn child." An odd beginning, but maybe not the least appropriate one for a young adult book writer.

I'd carved out my niche, but Ansbach was a grim posting. To make sure that we were all battle-ready, we were regularly called to mass formations at midnight and spent the time till breakfast scrubbing down the barracks. James Dean was done for, but the other great symbolic figure of my generation, Elvis Presley, was in the army then. He was posted elsewhere in Germany, but the newspapers were full of Elvis Serving His Country. Journalists seemed to believe that draftees could live in villas with their own servants when they were off duty. Elvis was delivered to his dayroom every morning in a splendid white Rolls-Royce and seemed to spend the rest of the day making movies in uniform, impersonating a soldier. The army made full use of him, but his special privileges had an adverse effect on the rest of us, and he was no hero to us.

Ansbach began to weigh heavy, and I looked around for advancement. One Sunday morning when I was sitting in the chapel, it struck me that we were hearing a sermon the chaplain had written back in his seminary days. That afternoon I went back to the barracks and wrote a sermon for soldiers, lonely ones a long way from home. Like a novel, a sermon needs to be for the congregation, not the preacher. I'd grown up in the Methodist church and knew my way around the Bible. And I could type.

I typed up a clean copy on the office machine and slid my sermon under the door of the chaplain's office. The next Sunday he delivered it from the pulpit. So I wrote him another. As I was handing in this one, I made sure he caught me.

"Soldier," he said, "how many of those sermons do you have?"

I told him that I had fifty-two a year, if I were chaplain's assistant. I hadn't been to chaplain's assistant school either, but then sermon-writing wasn't part of that job description, strictly speaking.

The chaplain was headed for a post at 7th Corps Headquarters in Stuttgart and took me with him. I cut my own travel orders and was on my way early in 1958. Ansbach had been a sleepy Hansel-and-Gretel kind of place glimpsed over the wall. Stuttgart was possibly the world's most modern city in the 1950s. Bombed flat in World War II, it had risen again as an industrial powerhouse, the home of Mercedes-Benz. It was a white city rising out of rose gardens in a valley surrounded by grape arbors and terraced restaurants, all rich beyond anything I'd seen in my own country.

My chaplain turned out to need more assistance than I'd foreseen. I extended my duties to conduct his marriage-counseling sessions. I expanded sermon-writing to include chaplains of all denominations. With a key to the chapel office, I spent the evenings there instead of the barracks. I was on call when the chaplains weren't. When soldiers saw a light in the chapel window, they'd come in and bring their troubles with them. I heard a lot of confessions. Maybe it was in the chapel basement where I learned that writing was going to be the art of listening.

My army days fell in the middle of that mandatory conscription era from the early forties until President Nixon ended it in 1973. We were mobilized a million strong in an era far more peaceful than now. What did we learn from this lavish expenditure of public money and our private lives?

It put a full stop to our adolescence. It cured some of us of communal living, conformist behavior, and dressing alike for the rest of our lives. It removed eighteen year olds from their mothers' houses to a world where beds don't make themselves. It introduced college grads to our first nonbenevolent power structure. The army overfed our youthful need for order, rules, strong codes. It made us hungrier for privacy and self-determination and saved most of us from the organized mass movements coming in the sixties. The army was a welfare state, and there we learned that welfare states are run for the convenience of the administrators, and not the needy. It taught me more than two years of college, and it brought me friends because the army's a place where you need them.

Carl Christoph from Morgantown, West Virginia, became a younger brother to me for the rest of his life. A musical genius from Port Arthur, Texas, John Ardoin, later went on to eminence as the biographer of Maria Callas. Jim Lumsden, the Los Angeles architect, became another brother to me. Calling ourselves "short-timers," we counted down the days till we could get out of the army and start our lives, and ever after we looked back, remembering the good times.

Six

CLASSROOMS

We were shooting along a highway through the biggest cemetery I ever saw. On both sides were thousands upon thousands of tombstones, jammed right up flush with each other. There wouldn't have been room to breathe, not that it matters. Awful, tacky plastic Christmas wreaths were leaning up on some of the stones, and the wind was whipping their ribbons. I hadn't known what to expect from New York City people, but I sure never knew most of them were dead.
— Representing Super Doll

Teaching was to me the art of the possible. Even if I'd thought there was a novelist in me, I'd come from Illinois where we were raised to make livings, not take chances. I chose teaching because I'd admired my teachers. They were the people interested in what interested me. Becoming a writer, I supposed, was the kind of thing that happens to somebody else, and in that I was right. I had to become someone else before I was ready to write: a teacher.

I entered the master's degree program at Southern Illinois University (SIU) in Carbondale. The assistantship to pay for it involved teaching two sections of freshman composition. The first class was to meet in three-hour sessions. Though the evening hour should have been a clue, I was just off a troop ship and still at sea in my native land.

On the long walk down the hall in a new civilian suit, I racked my brain to recall what I'd learned in those education courses. Did it have something to do with establishing my authority before the students established theirs? I could use grammar, but could I teach it? Like any beginning teacher, I thought I'd have to be the whole show, filling every minute. In this case, three hours.

Trying to look as old as possible, I entered the classroom to find I was the youngest person there. This was night school—adult education. The students were fully formed. They came across a dark and alien campus after work, hoping to start a college degree. They didn't notice I was young. Expecting a professor, they saw one.

I fell for teaching on the first night. There'd been life for these students before this classroom. They knew the value of a dollar and a day's work. They weren't kids. They were raising kids. There wasn't a tough cookie in the bunch. But they gave me endless trouble. Before every session, somebody was waiting in the hall, ready to drop the course. He was too old to be schooled. She'd never read anything worthwhile. He'd never been well spoken, and it was too late to change. She'd done the assignment, but couldn't understand it.

From them I learned the teacher's need to reassure. I wanted to tell them what I wasn't allowed to say, that I wouldn't be flunking anybody who tried. Which meant I wouldn't be flunking anybody. Never again was I to know students this vulnerable or punctual. One night Mr. Ginganbach barreled in an hour late. "I'd have been on time," he said, "but I had to take the wife to the labor room."

I taught for two years at SIU and another at Washington University in St. Louis, doing additional graduate work there. College teaching seemed a promising world then. We were still five years from the first student riots that struck college campuses in the late 1960s. But I went back to my original plan, to teach high school, one of those corners turned on the way to being a writer.

The high school was in a northern Chicago suburb so new the crab grass hadn't taken root. I never did. We teachers couldn't afford to live here, so our students saw us in the same light as the rest of the day-labor force who came in to do for them. These boys and girls—I'd left the world of men and women behind—weren't a lot younger than I was, but they were a different breed, my first suburbanites. In creeping stages, I learned that to them Chicago down the road was a remote place full of crime, confusion, and people beneath their social level. Here again I was to learn more than I taught.

It seemed to me that suburban life combined the disadvantages of urban and small-town life without the advantages of either. If there was a center at all, it was the high school itself, but here the students saw only each other. I wondered if they knew what their parents did for livings.

Having taken the job so I could live in Chicago, I decided to sell the city to my students. Vaguely, I remembered a professor in an education course who'd said, "A teacher is only as good as his bulletin boards." Acting on this ridiculous advice, I worked up a series of bulletin boards: one on the architectural glories of Chicago, another on a new Lyric Opera production, another on Carl Sandburg as Chicago poet so good you could have sold it as poster art.

One day after school a soft-spoken girl was watching me take down one bulletin board and put up another. Before drifting away, she said, "Gee, Mr. Peck, you sure do love your bulletin boards, don't you?"

I nearly swallowed my thumbtacks. She was right; I'd been doing them for myself. It was a lesson for teaching, for writing. Until you've found your way to your audience, you're talking to yourself.

The students in that school were strongly defended by peer-grouping, hair spray, and family money. I had to start over with them. Every parent expected college entrance for every child. If there was an alternative, it was socially unthinkable. The college counselor was the only visible faculty member in town. She outclassed the coach.

The teacher of senior-year English wasn't far behind. English teachers are thought to be able to phrase the best letters of recommendations to college admissions offices. In teaching the advanced placement seniors, I could hold this lightly over their heads, but I was never to maintain the standards of Miss F.

By declaring everybody college material, the school was based on an error. Most of its victims were invisible, and one of them lay comatose across the desk in a tenth-grade class of mine. He came alive, I'd heard, only in the industrial arts department, which in this school was only a holding tank for lost souls. His name was Scott, and I see him now as a heroic figure, the only student I knew who resisted the college-prep steamroller. He wasn't interested, and he wasn't preparing, and I didn't know what to do with him. I was sorely tempted to let him lie dormant since he wasn't giving trouble. Then one day I was heading through the parking lot past the MGs back to where the faculty parked. I'd outlived my Pontiac Catalina and sold short a '57 Chevy convertible before I found out it was going to be a classic. Now I was down to a Lark, the last gasp of the Studebaker company. Harder to deal with than any of my students, my old Lark wouldn't start. It often wouldn't and spent many a lonesome night in the school lot while I thumbed rides.

Scott appeared at my car window. The parking lot was his domain. He rapped on the glass, saying, "This yours? Jeez, a Studebaker. I might have figured. Raise your hood." He was under it quite a while, bad-mouthing my carburetor. "Gimme the keys," he said finally.

Scott gave the Lark the only expert tune-up it ever had. It made it through the year, and so did Scott. I tried to pay him for his labor, but he said, "What for? I don't pay you to teach me."

"I don't teach you anything," I said. But from that time on he let me teach him a little. I don't know what the moral of this story is. For pat endings, turn to television, not teaching.

That suburban school gave me a crash course in my own future. Now, most of the letters I receive from young readers bear suburban postmarks, and most of the school-visit invitations lead me to suburbia: Winnetka, Scarsdale, Northport, Encino, Shaker Heights. Suburbs are bigger now, cities smaller.

I set a number of my novels in suburbs, hoping to reach readers where most of them live, hoping to take them a step beyond. I think most families move to the suburbs, not to deal with life's problems, but to avoid them, like the families in Judith Guest's *Ordinary People* and in M. E. Kerr's *Night Kites*. There are people out there who believe they deserve a perfect existence because they paid so much for the house. There are young people who confuse suburban residence with academic giftedness.

Are You in the House Alone? is set in the suburbs. A novel about a rape victim might be set anywhere. Rape is our fastest-growing, least-reported crime, far more common now than in 1976 when the book was first published. The chief victim is a teenager, one of my readers perhaps, and so I placed her story in a suburb for a setting my readers couldn't distance themselves from and deny.

The novel isn't about rape. Young readers already know what that is. Instead, it points out that life is not a television show, with justice neatly delivered just before the final commercial. In our real-life implementation of the laws, the criminal regularly walks while the victim serves a kind of sentence. When the crime is rape, the sentence is for life.

For the young characters of the book, I researched a New Jersey community. The setting is a semifictitious town in Connecticut. A Rape Crisis Center on the North Shore of Chicago provided the profile of the young victim. Gail is a suburban high-school junior without street smarts or survival skills. When she's menaced by anonymous phone calls and letters, her judgment is blurred by the idealized setting of her town. She waits to be looked after. She actually opens the door when she's baby-sitting because she can't believe anybody she knows would hurt her. No one in her universe has told her that rapists are rarely strangers.

The rape scene doesn't appear in the book because I have ample respect for my readers' imaginations. The novel is instead about our response to victims, the attitudes of the police and the legal establishment, and most important to the victim, the attitudes of her friends. Gail's victimization disturbs their universe. She's alone in the end. The people around her want to put it all behind them, or blame her, while the rapist is given another chance. And takes it. No happy endings here, and it's by far my most widely read book, though many readers' letters remind me that I got the ending wrong.

I wrote the novel to point out that life is not a television show. It was made into a television show—aired in 1978. The film setting was vaguely Mill Valley, California, and not Connecticut, but that's close enough. The casting was excellent, though it includes a policewoman, which could raise false hopes in the reader. And of course it has a happy ending. Since a rapist needs to be caught in the act, Phil returns to attack Gail again, in the school darkroom where she can conveniently photograph him. The moral of the movie appears to be: keep your camera ready and hope your attacker doesn't mind providing evidence at his own trial. No, I had no control over the script. I first knew it was finished when I saw the listing in *TV Guide*.

Fifteen years have passed since *Are You in the House Alone?* was published, long before we'd heard the terms, "date rape" and "acquaintance rape." Now, police, hoping that victims can identify their attackers, ask them to look through the pictures in high-school and college yearbooks. More extreme than my fictional account. In 1976 a publisher in England rejected the book, pointing out that in that country rape is not a problem. A decade later when another British publisher, Pan Books, published it, *Are You in the House Alone?* was one of the hundred best-selling paperbacks in Great Britain.

Remembering the Good Times is another novel set in the suburbs. Different in tone and topic from *Are You in the House Alone?,* there are parallels. Both novels hope to raise questions and reveal what we know about current epidemics. By the mid-1980s the three great killers of teenagers were murder, drunken driving, and suicide. Epidemics on a scale we'd never seen before, and no Salk vaccine to fix them.

The novel deals with suicide, and I didn't lack sources for research. It's a problem coming partway out of the closet, acknowledged now by statisticians and journalists. But my readers don't read newspapers, and they go to schools where the telephone number of the local suicide crisis hotline isn't on the bulletin board. They come from homes where suicide isn't mentioned because "we don't have that kind of problem in our family." There are even parents who confuse suicide with sex and fear that if children find out what it is, they'll want to try it.

The book dramatizes the classic warning signs of teenaged suicide in the hope that someone somewhere might go for help, or help a friend. "He told us he was going to kill himself, but we didn't believe him" is a phrase that rings through our country. As with *Are You in the House Alone?*, I took the novel from life, embodying the human traits of the victim and of the people who love him from information given by suicide crisis hotline personnel.

The setting of *Remembering the Good Times* is an authentic country town merging into a subdivision of strangers. The suburban setting was inspired by Professor George Hendry of Princeton Theological Seminary who suggested as a root cause of our suicide rate the "easy life and empty optimism" of a generation left unchallenged. He cited the high suicide rates of Plano, Texas; Westchester County, New York; Beverly Hills, California—just the kinds of places my readers' letters come from.

Even very young people who kill themselves have long, undiagnosed histories. The events of the novel follow a four-year period, but it's his high school that pushes the main character, Trav, over the edge. He's a boy most likely to succeed, driven by a desperation masked by success. His school provides neither human shelter nor any real academic challenge. It moves at the pace of students who have their teachers thoroughly under control. Trav chooses death because he doesn't believe he's being prepared for the challenge of adult life.

At sixteen, he's out of reach. His young friends admire him too much to see his symptoms. His parents care, but he's rarely at home. He's well out of range of guidance counselors, who are geared to a far different, easier case load. As in most of my books, there's a wise, elderly woman in his life, Polly Prior, possibly my most successful character. But she's clinging to life at any cost. She can't imagine anyone as promising as Trav throwing away his life before it's begun. And so he slips away from us all, sped on his way by another model school in an ideally planned community.

I hope the novel is sound psychology, but it isn't meant to be amateur psychiatry. If we understood all we need to know about the impulses behind suicide, it wouldn't be sweeping a generation. But there are classic warning signs. In the book, Trav's closest friends, Buck and Kate, are only vaguely worried when, nearing his end, he gives them his treasured possessions. They're worried, but they don't act, as often happens in real life.

After Trav's death, there's a town meeting of the sort that happens in a novel and not in reality. But it was based on a real one, though the actual case was superficially different.

The meeting was held in the early eighties in a wealthy suburb after the death of a thirteen-year-old girl. She was new to the town and had been snubbed by her classmates at school.

She wasn't clean. She was incorrectly dressed, and they didn't know her. She'd been seen sitting alone in the town park during school hours, and she'd killed herself in her own home. In an earlier era, the local press might have suppressed this news, or rephrased it. But the story came out, occasioning a meeting.

The citizens talked, even debated for most of four hours. They didn't end the meeting until they were in agreement that their community provided more than adequate counseling and social services. Their conclusion was that the girl and her family were at fault for not availing themselves of help the community offered.

That meeting sparked the one in my book, altered by the addition of one woman who refuses to blame the victim in the interest of civic pride. A novel always has to offer that additional element that real life withholds.

Remembering the Good Times is the young adult book of my own that means the most to me. It's finding its way into classroom discussions, and the letters come. In a familiar pattern a lot of the readers say, "I loved the book but hated the ending. Trav shouldn't have killed himself." If he hadn't, of course, there'd have been no book, no need for it. I don't know how to answer these letters.

As blind to the future as usual, I moved on from my first high-school teaching post without knowing how large the suburban mind-set was going to loom in my future. I left without encountering as many parents as I'd have liked, and never the parents I needed to know. We were entering the era when teenagers can go off to school, secure in the knowledge that their parents and their teachers will never meet.

Now in novels for the children of my former students, the suburban settings are of a later generation, too. *Close Enough to Touch* is set in a suburb inspired by the one where I once taught, but updated. Suburbs have developed into less homogeneous communities than they intended to be. In this novel a boy from a working-class family living in a suburban apartment complex falls for a girl from the right end of town. He loses her, not to another boy, but to death.

It's another book that could be set anywhere, though it deals in the minute social distinctions made by young people more snobbish than their own parents. But the reason for the novel is to examine a teenaged boy's emotions. In losing the first girl he's ever loved, Matt thinks he's lost his only chance for happiness. It takes most of the book for him to give himself permission to cry, to grieve, and to begin again.

The emotional frigidity of boys and men arises in more than one novel of mine. I wrote this one to invite boys out of their shells, to express their emotions, not to fear them. Most of the letters that come about this book are from girls wanting to meet the boy in the book.

A brief, important scene in *Close Enough to Touch* needed the character of a teacher who could find the right words to help a frozen, grieving boy. I remembered a wonderful teacher I'd known at that suburban school, one from whom I'd learned a lot about teaching. In the novel, she's named Mrs. Tolliver. In real life, she's Ellie Dedrick.

Then, in 1965, I found myself in New York. Fate and my own instant nostalgia keep delivering me to places just as they're disintegrating.

I'd been waiting for the call to New York all my life. It finally came from the distinguished English department chairman of a school on Park Avenue. Evolved out of a college lab school, it now functioned for academically gifted girls. It was a school and an era that would make a writer out of me.

That first year was heavy with omens. The Great Blackout of November trapped the jammed subway car I just happened to be in for the five hours it took until we could be fished up, one at a time, through a manhole in front of City Hall.

The experience must have left its mark. In 1978, this paragraph appeared in *Father Figure*:

> We stop dead center in the middle of the East River tunnel. Complete power loss. Dead, underwater silence. The lights dim. Ocean-going vessels pass directly over our heads. Green Mafia corpses, scientifically weighted, graze the tunnel top with seaweed hands. Rats glance out from tile chinks at the sudden stillness of us be-calmed under water.

With the election of a Republican mayor, John Lindsay, the unions paralyzed the city with two weeks of strikes—and shut down the subway again.

Education for the gifted was an empire on the rise. My new school, grades seven through twelve, was devoted entirely to the presumed gifted. With a midwestern awe of New York, I wondered what I'd have to offer young geniuses sprouting in the rich cultural concrete of this city.

It was the time when Lincoln Center was rising out of urban renewal. Armies were massing to march against the Vietnam War. Thirteen-year-old girls, small as sprites, threaded through the baffles of a subway system, on their way to school. There was talk of consciousness-raising in the faculty lounge. When I arrived, the English department was removing a book from the curriculum and disposing of the class sets: Harper Lee's *To Kill a Mockingbird*. The reason given was that it celebrated white bourgeois values, which were the values of the people banning it, as far as I could tell.

New in town, I did the only thing I could think of. I wrote the title and author across the blackboard in my classroom. Then I told the students the simple truth, that *To Kill a Mockingbird* had been banned from their reading list for their own well-being. Though many of them appeared to be too gifted to read, they all read one book that semester.

Today, gifted programs are in full cry across the country, and I visit a number of them. Who can criticize a program that may in fact be the only literacy training offered in the school? But my experience in the New York school gave me reservations. To be labeled "gifted" too early in life causes most people to go out of business.

Once Margaret Mead came across the park from her office in the Natural History Museum to talk to our seniors. To the awe of the faculty, she strode in, wearing flowing tribal robes and carrying a Samoan chieftain's staff for a walking stick.

She spoke to our female students about her career, nearing its end, in anthropology, a field where a woman had to smooth her own way. She had the rare gift of combining scholarship with actual experiences laced with anecdotes. Her theme was that all people, and particularly women, have to prepare for two careers: the one they really want and the one they may need on the way to it. "Whether you want to be an anthropologist or an astronaut, nurses' training would be invaluable," she said. "And you'll need secretarial skills in every field. Rely upon your skills, not the skills of others. Be ready to do what you have to do."

But a student was on her feet in the audience. They weren't good listeners, and this one had heard enough. "Lady," she said, snapping her fingers to stem Margaret Mead's flow, "I don't think you know who we are. We aren't going to be secretaries. We're gifted."

My teaching ground to a halt in that school. History was catching up with the classroom. Peace rallies grew violent. There was racial unrest. The distance between word and deed yawned at our feet.

New York has always confused chaos with creativity, but there were opportunities. In fact, I may be the only person I ever knew who really was liberated by the late sixties. I learned more about the young now that they were less interested in a teacher's good opinion. Political activism, though it amounted mainly to running your mouth and cutting school, became the ideal adolescent mask for personal uncertainty. As the school caved in to each new demand, the students grew desperate, and we, the faculty, stood by, watching the world the young create when they can't count on us.

I quit teaching in that era when the parents and the teachers in my generation of people lost our way. When our children tested our standards for them, to see if we would stand firm, we crumbled. It was a massive failure of nerve that swept a generation of adults and has never been adequately explained.

Now, the generation I taught are the parents of my readers. In *Princess Ashley*, Chelsea's father is a Vietnam vet, still suffering. Pod's parents are old counterculturalists, "rich hippies," and so he has to find his maturity somewhere else.

On May 24, 1971, I left teaching. I turned in my tenure, my

hospitalization, my pension plan, and my attendance book, which was in fact the first work of fiction I ever wrote. I went home to write or die, sure I wouldn't teach again, convinced I couldn't do anything else. In those first quiet months, I learned that the only way you can write is by the light of the bridges burning behind you.

THE HOUSE IN THE ALLEY

I didn't know what to write about. I sure wasn't going to write about myself if I might have to read it out loud. But writing something or other every day got me into a rhythm. Mr. Mallory said if we got writer's block, we should make lists of vocabulary words we could draw on later. I made a lot of lists.

—Princess Ashley

I lived in an 1830s carriage house in a residential alley, a mews, in Brooklyn Heights. There was a fanlight over the door and a willow tree out back. The living room was the old hayloft with a grain chute down to the cellar horse stalls. Over the years, carriage houses along the alley had evolved into garages with limousines below and chauffeurs' apartments carved out of the lofts. The last remaining chauffeur and his wife lived just opposite. More New England than New York, Brooklyn Heights drew me because the streets were tree-lined like the middle west and led down to the Promenade with a spectacular view of Manhattan.

I've set few of my novels in the city where I've written them all. When I do, I'm liable to play the place for laughs as I did in *New York Time,* and with the trip Verna and Darlene take in *Representing Super Doll.*

Father Figure, though, is about a private-school boy and his little brother who've been growing up on Remsen Street around the corner from where I lived. The chauffeur's in it, too. I chose Brooklyn Heights because it sums up the stiff-necked traditions of the boys' grandmother, Grace Livingston. She sets the novel in motion by sending her grandsons away to spend a summer with the father they hardly know. After the death of her daughter, their mother, she knows she won't be able to bring them up. Though she's no friend of their father, she hopes he and his sons can build something together. It's a novel to find out if fathers and sons can be family for one another, and about the male problem of expressing emotions.

Once again, Hollywood was at the door, but the filmed version of *Father Figure* was reworked to feature, not the sons, but the father and Hal Linden who played him.

Still, the movie ends as the novel does. For the teenaged son and his father, too much time has been lost. Though Jim works through his anger at his dad, they have to part, guarded friends. In order to grow up, Jim has to make an unthinkable sacrifice that involves his little brother. My experiences with filmdom haven't been happy, but hearing the dialogue I'd written for Jim spoken by Timothy Hutton compensated. I went on to create Matt in *Close Enough to Touch* with Timothy Hutton in mind, but by that time he'd won an Oscar for his role in *Ordinary People* and had given up teenaged roles.

I found my third New York novel by looking out across my back garden into the windows of the tall old mansion where my landlords lived. I grow a little wary about describing the actual events that suggested it, but some of them can be figured out by reading *Through a Brief Darkness*.

My original landlords made an abrupt departure. We've all heard of tenants who skip out on landlords, but I was a tenant whose landlords had skipped. Very little about New York life bears any resemblance to America.

A more recent novel, *Voices After Midnight,* is set in New York, too, in another tall and mysterious townhouse, though it was inspired by E. Nesbit's English stories. The house is on East Seventy-third Street in Manhattan, around the corner from where I live now. Here a California family with three kids, Heidi, Chad, and Luke, come innocently to stay for a summer in crumbling New York. Some of them learn that in the old house if you open just the right door in just the right mood, it will be 1888 on the other side.

But these New York novels came later. On the evening of May 24, 1971, I returned home to the house in the alley, unemployed, to see if I could be a writer. The school I'd left behind had been unusual in combining junior high with high school. So without warning, I was a teacher of junior high with the age-old problem. I couldn't find relevant readings. *To Kill a Mockingbird* had already been banned, and you can get just so much mileage out of "The Red Pony."

Carson McCullers's *The Member of the Wedding* is still the best portrait of a girl at puberty I've ever read, but my students staged one of their readouts after they saw that Frankie Adams was no older, no wiser, no kinder than they were. Worse, at the end of the book, Frankie's still sunk in puberty, and help isn't on the way, or hope. It's a novel for adult survivors of puberty who dare to look back.

When I couldn't sell Frankie Adams to my students, it was

the last straw. That must have been the day that I made a commitment to being a writer myself.

While I was looking high and low for books my teenagers couldn't deny or disdain, another teenager out in Tulsa was writing *The Outsiders*. While I was the only one in the classroom not going through puberty, across the river in New Jersey Judy Blume was writing *Are You There God? It's Me, Margaret.* Paula Danziger was still teaching, and somewhere Robert Newton Peck was writing *A Day No Pigs Would Die,* a book I'd be credited with writing forever after.

A new publishing field was being born, "Young Adult." There in the wings were Paul Zindel, Robert Cormier, M. E. Kerr, but I didn't find them in time to rescue my reading curriculum. I only met up with them later because I couldn't find them as a teacher.

I owe a writing career to those junior-high students of mine. Only the pubescent could have driven me to this extreme. But in that first summer at the typewriter, I couldn't put on paper what I'd just observed in the classroom. I was still too near it.

For my first try, I turned instead to the experiences of my friends, Jean and Richard Hughes, who in those years took into their family in Evanston, Illinois, girls from a home for unwed mothers. At their house I'd met teenaged girls waiting to have their babies and facing the decisions to follow. With junior-high readers in mind, I began a story about an unwed mother.

Though I must have taught two-hundred novels, writing a single short one posed sudden difficulties. In the long run, it turned out to be the easiest to write because I never had to stop and ask, "Have I written these words before? Am I on a roll, or am I repeating myself?"

But the eternal problem of viewpoint came up. I'd taught

viewpoint; now I learned what it is. I thought I'd have to let the unwed mother tell her own story, but somehow she couldn't, or wouldn't.

In the center of a city full of the employed, I sat out in that hot garden under a weeping willow tree, stuck on page forty. Finally, it occurred to me. I wasn't on her side. Being pregnant, she had an entire social-services system to prop her up, a case worker, a group home to go to, a family to take her in. Care-givers buzzed around her. It was guidance counselors' mate-rial. As a classroom teacher, I'd been more worried about the quiet kids, often on the back row, with problems far more sub-tle and harder to treat.

Starting over, I told the unwed mother's story from her youn-ger sister's viewpoint, a girl who isn't in the kind of trouble adults can no longer overlook. When her big sister leaves with-out a backward glance to have her baby, Carol has to find a way to hold the family together, to be responsible for herself and others. The novel became *Don't Look and It Won't Hurt* and sold a half million copies.

I'd entered teaching in order to teach composition, writing. I left it in search of readings I couldn't find for my students. What had I learned to make writing my own books possible?

For one thing, neither a teacher nor a book dares talk down to the young. And so I wasn't going to tack on happy endings that insult readers' intelligence, even though they cry out for happy endings.

A writing colleague, Blossom Elfman, has an anecdote from her teaching days in a school for teenaged unwed mothers. She took a group of them to see Franco Zeffirelli's film of *Romeo and Juliet*. They were spellbound by the lush glamor, the flow of poetry, the young Romeo. But at the end they staged an insurrection. "You didn't tell us they *kill them-selves*," they said, stalking back on the bus.

In not talking down to anybody, I knew I wasn't going to control the vocabulary of my novels. As any teacher knows, there's no such thing as a "grade reading level." The reading rate of everybody in the room rose and fell according to degree of interest, including mine. A novel is an opportunity to learn new vocabulary, the only opportunity when teachers aren't handing out word lists and students don't have to report to class with dictionaries in hand.

Using the language I hear from the young won't work either. In *Representing Super Doll*, if Darlene the beauty queen had told her own story, it would have run to eight-hundred pages, consisting mainly of three words, *like* and *you know*. For *Representing Super Doll*, I had to find a more articulate, less realistic narrator.

I'd learned a lot by trying to teach *The Member of the Wedding* to a room full of Frankie Adamses. The main characters of my novels were going to have to be not only a little older, but able to do something the readers can't.

In a book of light reading, the characters may be able to travel in time, see ghosts, slay dragons, be Cinderellas of both sexes. In books of more serious intent, they are going to take a step forward toward maturity, even now when maturing itself has become an elective.

In time that led to *Princess Ashley*, a novel on the theme that most impressed me as a teacher: the now unshakable power of the adolescent peer group and what it does with that power. A high-school girl, Chelsea, believes her mother is never right, while the girl who commands her peer group at school is never wrong. From Ashley, Chelsea takes commands she wouldn't accept from the mother who loves her. Ashley loves only herself, a signal trait for a teen leader, and she knows how to create willing handmaidens. Chelsea spends most of her high-school life belonging instead of becoming.

Then the novel departs from reality as novels must. In real life, she'd go on to pledge Kappa at State U. In the novel, she finally sees what her leader is and revolts. Better yet, she declares her independence in time for a senior year she can plan for herself.

In shedding Ashley, Chelsea begins to learn one of life's hard skills, how to walk away:

> In a way—not the old way—I didn't want her to go. I wanted to call her back so we could end our friendship. But there was nothing to end. I just kept walking. There was nothing to it. And I didn't look back in case she waved.

This hard-edged novel about how the young use each other and how the loneliness of independence is worth it has been surprisingly popular. But letters come from junior-high readers who prefer the manipulative and possibly psychotic Ashley. A direct quote from a letter: "I loved Ashley. She reminds me of my best friend. We do everything together."

Was it in the classroom I learned that when I said one thing, they heard another?

Teaching even found me a publisher. In that last school I'd collaborated with a colleague, Ned Hoopes, on an anthology of contemporary nonfiction. We needed a sound, representative, fifty-cent paperback collection for the classroom, and we did one, called *Edge of Awareness,* for our own students. It was published by Dell Publishing Company. It's still in print a quarter of a century later, though not at fifty cents. And the book we did for tenth graders now sells almost exclusively to college classes.

At Dell I met a young editor, George Nicholson, with a bright future in the field. Toward the end of 1971 when I'd reworked my first novel six times, I took it to him in a shoe box. By then he was juveniles editor-in-chief at Holt, Rinehart & Winston. He took *Don't Look and It Won't Hurt* for a reading, called me at eight-thirty the next morning, and said, "You can start your second novel." At Holt and then Viking and then back at Delacorte/Dell, George Nicholson has published all my young adult novels.

Teaching had made this new career possible, but it hadn't taught me how to sit alone in an empty room without bells. I missed the shape of the school day. I missed colleagues and young voices. In teaching, there's always someone there to blame.

I had to learn to sit by myself and create company on the page. "I love being a writer," Peter De Vries said. "What I can't stand is the paperwork." The book characters weren't going to be any more tractable than students, and I'd catch myself delivering whole lessons aloud. Teaching's a job you never really quit; you just go on and on, trying to turn life into lesson plans. I used that. I began to think of chapters with the same attention span as class periods, to think of novels as lesson plans in the guise of entertainment. I supposed I'd have to sit home from now on to get the books written.

It wasn't to be, and it wouldn't have worked. With a launching from the publisher, I began to have invitations to speak to librarian and teacher groups. Schools began to invite young adult writers to come and meet with young people.

As with teaching, I'd backed into a field without knowing anything about it, but it made sense. My young readers don't read reviews, and neither they nor their teachers send off for the catalogs the publishers produce at great expense. Writers have to go out to tell readers about their books, and gather material for the next one.

I'd done only a book and a half when I was invited to pinch-hit as a speaker for the Indiana Library Association. I wrote out every word of the speech and rehearsed it for a month. In Indianapolis, I met up with my old fraternity brother, Gayle Byers, and his wife, Jane. True blue, they came to the speech and counted the house. It was a full program, and I didn't speak until nine P.M., following a dinner, a woman who sang *The Lord's Prayer,* and a steak-knife raffle.

During the last rehearsal of the speech in the hotel room, I'd realized I didn't know a word of it. But I'd written it all out, as I still do, and could read it if I had to. At 9:45 on the podium when I came to the conclusion, I glanced down to see that I'd never turned over a page of the script. I'd subconsciously memorized it all, and adrenaline did the rest.

Out in the milling lobby afterward, Jane Byers said, "Wait here. I'm going into the powder room to hear how you did."

I fell for public speaking just as I'd fallen for teaching, on the first night. Being a writer was to take me far from the house in the alley, and to fulfill that other early dream of going everywhere. I was going to see classrooms and school libraries in places I'd never heard of, and find ideas I could never have thought of. It would be teaching without tears. I don't have to grade anybody.

These school visits spark ideas that find their way into my novels. Sometimes I read aloud an early scene of a novel in progress, then ask a group of young readers how I should end it. In a place called Ridgway, Colorado, I read the beginning of what was to be *Close Enough To Touch*.

The opening scene sounds like the closing scene of a romance. Matt's finally worked up the courage to say to Dory, "I love you." She has her reply ready: "What took you so long?" The students liked that. There was a deer in the first scene, struck down by a car. Since they were Coloradans, it suggested to them that the novel took place where they lived. Then I said, "You won't see this girl again. She dies, and so Matt has to learn how to deal with his grief, his emotions."

They were startled by that, sitting forward. "What do you think he can do to ease his pain?" I asked.

After a silence, a boy said, "He could kill himself."

I was suddenly a teacher again, hearing an answer I didn't want. Suicide as a solution? No, I couldn't handle that, and I fumbled for answers.

I was still looking for those answers later in my novel *Remembering the Good Times*. It was a book initiated by a boy in a school in the Colorado mountains, responding to a question.

On the road, I came to know that these responses to one novel led on to the next one. I'd worried about where the next book idea would come from, but now I knew to keep asking questions with a notebook ready.

In my travels I wanted to find young writers, too. From teaching, I'd learned that some of them would write down what they wouldn't say aloud. On occasion I'll visit with students who've written a paper for me to read in advance. In reading them, I catch glimpses of these authors before we meet. Then when we do, I ask the author of the paper I thought was best to read it aloud. Usually, it's an outsider. Authors are.

The paper I ask students to write is called "Something That Happened to Me That Would Fit into a Novel."

It's an assignment that might invite self-involved self-expression, but most of the writing is about other people: younger siblings and younger selves, the deaths of grandparents and increasingly the deaths of older brothers and sisters in drunken driving. Drugs are more taboo as subject matter to the young than to the rest of us because they see more of it. No paper has ever touched on the power of the peer group, another topic too touchy. In fact, none of the papers ever mention school at all, as if their writers stop living during the day.

In Alaska you get a lot of stories about fish that got away and the night the bear got on the roof. In California a lot about life after parental divorce, and the most popular setting coast-to-coast is the shopping mall. One in a hundred papers is a comic tale, always by a boy. One in ten is a hard-to-believe revision of a Harlequin romance, always by a girl. Then there are the people who won't play fair. There are eighth-grade boys who write endless science fiction tales. Something that happened to *them* that would fit into a novel? No, but they're in the depths of puberty, and they aren't talking. Stories to them are only for escape, and the farther the better.

It's a factor I have to reckon with as their writer. I'm moved, too, to write what they won't because I don't really believe that the most dramatic thing that ever happened to them was a fish, an extraplanetary experience, a visit to Disney World back in third grade, or something that in fact happened to somebody else.

Unfinished Portrait of Jessica is a novel inspired by one of these student compositions. I wrote it about what the young writer had left out in describing her anger at her mother for not being able to hold her father, in her anger at him for marrying again. The writer of that paper was nearing senior year, but still she hadn't moved beyond blame-shifting. Her paper burned with anger and self-pity. It seemed to me she was about to enter an adult world in which all women are the enemy and all men are just going out the door. I wrote my novel about a girl who moves beyond this to a better place.

Does she live happily ever after? No, nobody does. All my novels end at a new beginning after one necessary step forward.

I see more writing from young people than I ask for. They often send me their work and ask my advice. There may just be more aspiring young authors out there than readers. "There are three rules for writing," Somerset Maugham said. "Unfortunately no one knows what they are." Still, I'm so often asked for advice that I've worked up a response. It's no foolproof formula because there aren't any, but I believe in it:

To Aspiring Writers

1. Never write what you know. Write what you can find out. If you're writing research papers that have to be footnoted, you're on the way to fiction writing because all fiction has to be documented, too, on every page in the lives of the readers.

2. Words are the bricks of your writing, and you need a larger supply than you have. If your teachers of all subjects aren't providing specialized vocabulary lists to be memorized, ask them why not.

3. Fiction is strongly based on the search for roots. Most stories are family stories. Take time out from avoiding your parents to find out who they are.

4. Fiction is never about ordinary people. For subject matter, look around for the people in your school who aren't full-time conformists.

5. Write each page at least six times. Professional writers are just like students. We never get anything right in the first five tries either. If your teachers are willing to give grades on rough drafts, ask them to rethink their position.

6. Read a book a week to see how other people do it. Writing is hard enough without the help and inspiration of your fellow writers.

7. Writing requires as much practice as the piano and more than football. Carve out the time from television and spend an hour a day writing.

8. Finally, think of all writing as communication, not self-expression. Nobody in the world wants to read your diary—except your mother.

INSPIRATIONS

This Gift has its drawbacks, but then I've always had a full share of drawbacks myself. Though the past and future are often open books to me, I have more trouble than most getting through the present.

—Blossom Culp
and the Sleep of Death

People are always asking authors where we get our book ideas. Some people even think we have a secret source and won't reveal it. We don't—I don't, and so I'm always on the lookout. To me, writing a novel is like making a quilt (though I've never made a quilt). You gather bright scraps from other people's lives and then stitch them together in a pattern of your own.

An anonymous girl's angry, anguished writing in response to my assignment inspired *Unfinished Portrait of Jessica*. It was one letter too many with the phrase, "Today after school, when we got to the mall. . . " that instigated *Secrets of the Shopping Mall*.

The names of characters: Matt, Ashley, Chad, Jessica, Rusty, Brooke, Trav, Heidi, Drew, Heather, Stephanie, came from the signatures on readers' letters. All the ethnic names come from the Brooklyn phone book, and some of the parental ones from my high-school yearbook.

I saw Pod, a character in *Princess Ashley* who gets some reader mail of his own, with my own eyes. During the Southern Methodist University Literary Festival, a young man entered a freshman class, wearing snow-white Levis, starched white cowboy shirt, and a white plastic cap labeled "Peterbilt." He gave the classroom a sweeping girl-check and took a full four minutes to get from door to desk, so studied his western walk, so cool his every move. Before he got there, I'd nailed him for the novel.

I met Madam Malevich having tea in the Astor Hotel in London. My editor George Nicholson, my friend Jack Cook, and I were there after a matinee, and there was a woman holding court across the room. Her gestures were from grand opera, her profile an eagle's, her hair raven black. When we got up to go, I said to George, "Notice the woman on the banquette. She's a gem."

He turned to look. She looked up. "George!" she shrieked.

"Dagmar!" he replied. Which really irritated me. George knows everybody.

She was Dagmar Godowsky, whose memoirs Viking had published. In her youth she'd made movies with Rudolph Valentino. We gave her a dinner party where she presided and regaled a long table of British publishers. Though she didn't live much longer, she lives on as Madam Malevich in *Are You in the House Alone?* She's someone else in the book, an elderly drama teacher, an eccentric in a suburb that can't pigeonhole her, and the only person in town who understands the young.

> We knew, too, that, crackpot though she was, she observed us with a sharp eye, in between bouts of vagueness. Most of the kids thought she was actually crazy, but I never did.
>
> And always before her monologue rambled on to the theater or film-making, she'd hit us with the one-liner to bring us down in a heap: "My God, all so young and so lifeless. At your age already I was *somebody*!"

In *Remembering the Good Times*, Kate's great-grandmother is Polly Prior, a very old woman being young one last time with the young people gathered in her kitchen around her. She is Blossom Culp, grown old, but still herself. Even our characters provide us with characters.

The Hughes family's work with unwed mothers inspired my first book, *Don't Look and It Won't Hurt,* and in one way or another they have been instrumental in all the rest. The most graphic scene in *Are You in the House Alone?* is a rape victim's physical examination. A necessary scene since most rape victims don't go for medical attention. It had to be right, but I'm no doctor. Richard Hughes is, and his understanding goes well beyond the medical. He talked me through a pelvic examination and corrected the errors once I'd written it. The book is dedicated to him, with reason.

All fiction is based on research. If I were limited to writing what I know, I'd have produced in all these years one unpublishable haiku. Like a teacher, a writer can't be the whole show if he expects to be heard.

When I needed a divorce, for *New York Time,* I applied to my agent, Sheldon Fogelman, who's a lawyer. Given the divorce rate among my readers, I needed an authentic one, and he was able to call down the right volume of Illinois divorce law so that my two characters could part realistically.

When it came time to write *Princess Ashley,* Jean and Richard Hughes's younger daughter, Courtney, was a teenager. For the book, I wanted a photographically real high-school backdrop and all its social implications. Courtney, served as my mole. She had a writer's own way of being there and yet looking on. Then she'd discreetly graduated before the book was published. It's dedicated to her and to Aaron and Ann Biggers who provided insights of another high school from a teacher's point of view.

Publishers inspire, too. Some people wonder if they tell authors what to write about, but that hasn't happened to me, exactly. Once, though, when a former paperback publisher and I were on a publicity tour in California, she said, casually, "You could write a novel for adults."

"No, I couldn't," I said. "I have enough to do, and I don't know anything about adult readers."

"It would have to be eight-hundred manuscript pages long, and historical," she said. "Nobody wants a short historical novel."

"I've never written eight-hundred pages of anything, not even if you added up all my books," I said, which was true at the time. "Even if you added letters home."

The publisher seemed not to hear me. "If you were to write a big historical novel," she said, "what would it be about?"

"Oh well, that's easy," I said. "It would be about everybody's favorite disaster, the sinking of the *Titanic.*" It had been all those junior-high boys who let me know that the *Titanic* is still afloat in the public imagination.

"That'll be fine," she said. "Give me fifty pages and an outline. I'll have the contract waiting in New York when we get home."

I spent the next four years writing a historical novel. I thought I'd never see the end of it. I thought it would be unpublishable. It was called *Amanda/Miranda,* and sold in eight languages and braille.

I lived for four years with the deck plan of the *Titanic* taped to my study wall, and then turned to the two other books for my fellow adults, *New York Time,* and another historical novel, a multigenerational epic called *This Family of Women.*

A reader of *Amanda/Miranda,* Isabelle Daniels Griffis—who is ninety this year—had sent me her Pasadena mother's notes on the tragic story of the pioneer Oatman family. I wove the events of old times and historic figures into *This Family of Women,* trying to blend the real and storytelling.

On the January day in 1990 when I heard I'd won the American Library Association's Author Achievement Award for Young Adult writers, I was in the third lock of the Panama Canal. By then, I'd begun to spend part of the year on an ocean liner, giving a course in creative writing to the passengers, lecturing on our ports of call.

A ship full of passengers is like a school full of students, everybody dressed alike and waiting for lunch. In the generation of cruise-ship passengers I met the grandparents of my teenaged readers and found them more frank then the parents.

As a member of the ship's staff, I could sit backstage during the shows, hearing the comedian warm up, watching the magician ready his rabbit, hearing the sidelong comments of bespangled show girls. Of course there was a novel in it, and backstage I met the famous big band singer from the 1940s, who became Connie Carlson, Drew and Steph's grandmother in *Those Summer Girls I Never Met.* Life has cast me in odd roles, and I've found myself conducting large parties of passengers through the ironclad customs shed at the port of Leningrad. The itinerary of that trip becomes the voyage in *Those Summer Girls I Never Met,* and the Russian scene is adapted from a real-life incident.

In the winter season of 1989–1990 when we were anchored at Acapulco, I found above a bay outside the city a house up in the rocks that became the setting for *Unfinished Portrait of Jessica*.

In 1990 I visited eighteen countries and crisscrossed my own. Visiting the American International Schools in Vienna and Budapest took me to Hungary in its first months of freedom. Back in 1956, the army had threatened us with Hungary, and here I was at last, rolling over the border in a parlor car, the only American in an invading force of Japanese businessmen.

It's the age of the portable author, though long before our time, Charles Dickens traveled himself to death as a platform speaker. I have enough frequent flyer miles to circle the moon, and I spend a little lifetime in airports. It was a scene in the Miami airport that provided the last page of *Father Figure*.

Passengers don't converse much on airplanes anymore. Still, on the business flights, I'm occasionally asked what I do for a living. I used to come clean and say I was a writer.

This didn't work out. People said, "Would I have read anything you've written?"

The only answer to that is, "I don't know. How well read are you?"

When they heard I wrote for the young, the problem deepened. "My children love to read," says someone's dad.

But when I'd ask what they were reading, Dad never knew. In flight is no place for a sermonette about how reading the books his children read can open doors between them. Nowadays when I'm asked what line of work I'm in, I say, "publishing."

"Sales?" I'm asked, and I nod, hoping it's true.

EPILOGUE

Then me and Alexander Armsworth
walked out into the bright November
morning, almost hand in hand.
 —The Dreadful Future
 of Blossom Culp

A more complete autobiography would be written on the deathbed, but as I'm currently in the midst of a three-book contract, I have miles to go before I sleep. Still, I'm old enough to look back, and to pay more attention to what people do than what they say. Old enough to know who my friends are and to know that reading has seen us all through a great deal.

I loved history before I had one. Whatever else happens to us, we're informed by the era, the decade when we came of age. That's why communicating with you who are reading these words has always seemed the job most worth doing.

It's a field in which nobody wants to see my transcript, and nobody cares where I went to college, or if. And while I was never in the gifted program, it's just as well because in real life, there is no gifted program.

A writer can't help but divide all the world he knows between readers and nonreaders. I can only reach for the readers, and through them, the future.

I conclude, then, in the voice of a young reader.

I READ

I READ: because one life isn't enough, and in the pages of a book I can be anybody;

I READ: because the words that build the story become mine, to build my life;

I READ: not for happy endings but for new beginnings; I'm just beginning myself, and I wouldn't mind a map;

I READ: because I have friends who don't, and young though they are, they're beginning to run out of material;

I READ: because every journey begins at the library, and it's time for me to start packing;

I READ: because one of these days I'm going to get out of this town, and I'm going to go everywhere and meet everybody, and I want to be ready.

PUBLISHED WORKS

Novels for Young Readers

1972 *Don't Look and It Won't Hurt,* Holt, Rinehart, & Winston.

1973 *Dreamland Lake,* Holt, Rinehart, & Winston.

1973 *Through a Brief Darkness,* Viking.

1974 *Representing Super Doll,* Viking.

1975 *The Ghost Belonged to Me,* Viking.

1975 *Ghosts I Have Been,* Viking.

1976 *Are You in the House Alone?,* Viking.

1978 *Father Figure,* Viking.

1979 *Secrets of the Shopping Mall,* Delacorte.

1981 *Close Enough to Touch,* Delacorte.

1983 *The Dreadful Future of Blossom Culp,* Delacorte.

1985 *Remembering the Good Times,* Delacorte.

1986 *Blossom Culp and the Sleep of Death,* Delacorte.

1987 *Princess Ashley,* Delacorte.

1988 *Those Summer Girls I Never Met,* Delacorte.

1989 *Voices After Midnight,* Delacorte.

1991 *Unfinished Portrait of Jessica,* Delacorte.

Novels for Adults

1980 *Amanda/Miranda,* Viking.
1981 *New York Time,* Delacorte.
1983 *This Family of Women,* Delacorte.

Picture Book

1977 *Monster Night at Grandma's House* (illustrated by Don Freeman), Viking.

Nonfiction Anthologies

1966 *Edge of Awareness* (co-edited with Ned E. Hoopes), Dell Laurel Leaf.
       Leap into Reality.

Verse Anthologies

       Sounds and Silences
       Mindscapes
       Pictures That Storm Inside My Head